A Garden of Flowers

All 104 Engravings from
the *Hortus Floridus* of 1614

TWO VOLUMES BOUND AS ONE

Crispin van de Pass

Dover Publications, Inc.
Mineola, New York

Bibliographical Note

A Garden of Flowers: All 104 Engravings from the Hortus Floridus *of 1614*, first published in 2002, is an unabridged republication of Book 1 and Book 2 of the 500-copy limited edition of *Hortus Floridus*, published in 1928 and 1929, respectively, by The Cresset Press Limited, London. This Dover reprint, which consists of the two volumes bound as one, includes the Prefaces by Eleanour Sinclair Rohde, the calligraphy by Margaret Shipton, and the text translated from the Latin by Spencer Savage, all from the Cresset Press edition. The collection of engravings reproduced here was originally produced in 1614 by Crispin van de Pass, and printed in 1615 in Utrecht, Holland by Salomon de Roy.

DOVER *Pictorial Archive* SERIES

Library of Congress Cataloging-in-Publication Data

Passe, Crispijn van de, d. 1670.
    [Hortus floridus. English]
    A garden of flowers : all 104 engravings from the Hortus floridus of 1614 / Crispin van de Pass.
        p. cm.
    Originally published as a two volume work: London : Cresset Press, 1928–1929.
    ISBN 0-486-42305-0 (pbk.)
    1. Flowers—Pictorial works. 2. Botanical illustration. 3. Passe, Crispijn van de, d. 1670.
4. Flowers—Early works to 1800. 5. Engraving, Dutch. I. Title.

SB407 .P3713 2002
635.9'022'2—dc21

                      2002067847

Manufactured in the United States of America
Dover Publications, Inc., 31 East 2nd Street, Mineola, N.Y. 11501

Contents

Meridies

HORTUS FLORIDUS
BY
CRISPIN DE PASS

DOVER PUBLICATIONS, INC.

HORTUS FLORIDUS

THE FIRST BOOK

Contayninge a very lively and true Description of the Flowers of the Springe. By

CRISPIN VAN DE PASS

With a preface by ELEANOUR SINCLAIR ROHDE and calligraphy by MARGARET SHIPTON.

Thy wearied mynde with other's paines
Come recreate and see
How lively Nature's growth [by Arte]
Presents itself in thee.

THE BOOKE TO HIS READERS

Come hither you that much desire
Rare flowers of dyvers Landes
I represent the same to you,
Set done unto your handes.
In perfect shape, and faire:
And also teach to colour them
Not missinge of a haire
Vsinge such coloures as requires
A master workman's will.
Not swervinge thence in any case
Declaringe there his skill.
Each flower his proper lineament
Presents from top to toe:
And shewes both Root, budd, blade and stalke
So as each one doth grow
Sparing no paines, nor charge I have,
Each seasons flower to passe:
In Winter, Somer, Springe and fall
Until this compleate was.
Now use this same for thy delight
Injoy it as thou wilt
Of blotts and blurrs most carefully
Restraine, or else 'tis spilt.

THOMAS WOOD

FINIS

PREFACE

The seventeenth century saw the production of many books of plant engravings, and of these the *Hortus Floridus* [1] of Crispin de Pass is generally acknowledged to be the masterpiece. The author, "Crispin de Pass the Younger" as he is described on the title-page of his book, came of a family of celebrated engravers. According to Wurzbach [Niederlandisches Künstler-Lexicon], he was born in 1589 and therefore he was 25 when the *Hortus Floridus* was published. The *Hortus Floridus* is really a Florilegium and its facination for garden lovers is due not only to the beauty of the engravings but also to the fact that the flowers depicted have been prime favourites in our gardens for over three centuries. The woodcuts in the works by the great botanists of the sixteenth century—Brunfels, Fuchs, and Mattioli—reached the high water mark of woodcut botanic illustration, but, as Mr. Savage has emphasised, they lacked the subtle effects of atmosphere. This a copper-plate engraver as skilled as Crispin de Pass achieved with brilliant success, and for three centuries his book has been a source of delight to garden lovers. The year after its publication in Latin the *Hortus Floridus* was "faithfully and truly translated out of the Netherlandish Originall into English" with the following title.

A Garden of Flowers, Wherein very lively is contained a
true and perfect Discription of all the Flowers contained in

[1] For full bibliographical details see "The *Hortus Floridus* of Crispijn Vande Pas the Younger" by S. Savage, Transactions of the Bibliographical Society.

these foure followinge bookes. As also the perfect true manner of colouringe the same with theire naturall coloures, being all in theire seasons the most rarest and excellentest flowers that the world affordeth; ministringe both pleasure and delight in the spectator and most especially to the well affected practisioner. All which to the great charges and almost incredible laboure and paine, the diligent Authore by foure yeares experience, hath very Laboriously compiled, and most excellently performed; both in their perfect Lineaments in representing them in theire coper plates: as also after a most exquisite manner and methode in teachinge the practisioner to painte them even to the liffe. Faithfully and truely translated out of the Netherlandish originall into English for the comon benefite of those that understand no other languages, and also for the benefite of others, newly printed both in the Latine and French tongues all at the Charges of the Author. Printed at Utrecht by Salomon de Roy, for Crispin de Pass, 1615.

The Spring Garden which forms the first part of *Hortus Floridus* contains a notable collection of engravings of spring flowers which are now established favourites, but many of which had only been introduced towards the close of the sixteenth and during the early years of the seventeenth century.

The tulips, auriculas, crown imperials and so forth which are familiar to every cottager to-day were rarities then and treasured as though they were jewels.

No flower perhaps has caused a greater sensation amongst gardeners and plant-lovers than the tulip when it was first introduced into western Europe. Of its history before 1550 we know nothing. It was certainly cultivated before that date in Turkey, but for how long we do not know. Busbequius the ambassador of the Emperor Ferdinand 1 to the Sultan mentions in a letter written in 1554 that he saw tulips flowering in a garden between Adrianople and Constantinople. "As we passed we saw everywhere abundance of flowers, such as the Narcissus, Hyacinths, and those called by the Turks Tulipan, not without great astonishment on account of the time of the year, as it was then the middle of winter, a season unfriendly to flowers. Greece abounds with Narcissus and Hyacinths, which have a remarkably fragrant smell; it is indeed so strong as to hurt those that are not accustomed to it. The Tulipan however have little or no smell but are admired for their beauty and variety of colour. The Turks pay great attention to the cultivation of flowers, nor do they hesitate, though by no means extravagant, to expend several aspers for one that is beautiful. I received several presents of these flowers, which cost me not a little." The first to record seeing a tulip flowering in western Europe was Conrad Gesner the botanist who, in 1559, saw them growing in a garden at Augsburg. In his *De Hortis Germaniae* he says "In this year of our Lord 1559 at the beginning of April in the garden of the ingenious and learned Councillor John Henry Herwart I saw there a plant which had sprung from seed which had been procured from Byzantia, or as some say from Cappadocia. It was growing with one large reddish flower, like a red lily, having eight petals of which four are outside, and just as many within, with a pleasant smell, soothing and delicate, which soon leaves it."

Before 1582 tulips had been introduced into England for Richard Hakluyt in his *Remembrances of Things to be Endeavoured at Constantinople* says "And now within these four years there have been brought into England from Vienna in Austria divers kinds of flowers called Tulipas, and these and others procured thither a little before from Constantinople by an excellent man called M. Carolus Clusius." Although nearly forty years before the outbreak of the remarkable tulip mania the great Belgian botanist de l'Escluse who had settled down in Leiden as Professor of Botany in 1593 was making a modest fortune by selling his bulbs. According to Nicolas Wassenaer [*Historisch Ver-Dael* 1625] de l'Escluse also introduced the Hyacinth of Peru and the Crown Imperial. By 1623 tulips had become the rage and this same author records that in 1623 a variety called *Semper Augustus* sold for 'thousands of florins' and that in 1625 an owner refused an offer of three thousand florins for two bulbs. In Paris tulips were the flowers most favoured by ladies to wear in their low cut dresses and gifts of the rarest were esteemed as though they were costly jewels. Parkinson in his *Paradisus* [1629] describes flower lovers as being 'more delighted in the search, curiosity, and rarities of these pleasant delights, then any age I thinke before. But indeede, this flower, above many other, deserveth his true commendations and acceptance with all lovers of these beauties, both for the stately aspect, and for the admirable varieties of colours, that daily doe arise in them.... But above and beyond all others, the Tulipas may be so matched, one colour answering and setting of another, that the place where they stand may resemble a piece of curious needle-work, or a piece of painting: and I have knowne in a Garden, the Master as much commended for this artifical form in placing the colours of Tulips, as for the goodnesse of his flowers or any other thing.... But to tell you of all the sorts of Tulipas [which are the pride of delight] they are so many, and as I may say, almost infinite, doth both passe my ability and as I believe the skill of any other...... Besides this glory of variety in colours that these flow-ers have, they carry so stately and delightfull a forme, and do abide so long in their bravery [enduring above three whole moneths from the first unto the last] that there is no Lady or Gentlewoman of any worth that is not caught with this delight or not delighted with these flowers."

By 1634 the tulip mania [1] in the Netherlands had reached such a pitch that the trade in the bulbs had become a mere gamble. Collegiums or Clubs were formed and held at the inns which became Tulip exchanges. A rare print of this period entitled "The Fools Wagon" satirised the mania

[1] For details of the tulip mania see article by W.S. Murray. Journal of the Royal Horticul-tural Society. March 1909.

by showing a chaise-like car with Flora holding in one hand a horn of plenty containing tulip blooms and in the other three separate blooms. Three florists with her named "Good for Nothing" "Eager Rich" and "Tippler" are decked with tulips. A crowd runs after the car trampling on their weaving looms etc: and calling out "We will all sail with you". By 1637 the tulip mania which had attracted countless ne'er do wells and ruined thousands was at an end, but 1733 and 1734 witnessed a mild revival of the mania and even as late as 1836 16,000 francs [£650] was paid for a new tulip, the "Citadel of Antwerp" by an Amsterdam amateur.

De l'Escluse to whom tulip lovers owed so much was also chiefly responsible for the introduction of the auricula. It was only towards the close of the sixteenth century that the beauty of the alpine flora first attracted the serious attention of botanists and gardeners. When de l'Escluse accepted the invitation of the Emperor Maximilian II [himself a great garden lover] to Vienna and was made Court botanist he found the Viennese ladies enthusiastic gardeners, the market where roots of alpine flowers were sold being largely patronised by them. De l'Escluse spent many years at Vienna [1573-1587] and it was during this period that he so frequently climbed the peaks in the Tyrol and Styria in search of fresh treasures. He had a special affection for the genus primula and devoted much attention to naturalising *p. auricula* and *p. glutinosa* in his garden. He gave the name *auricula ursi* to these species owing to the resemblance of the leaves to bears ears [hence "sanicle"]. Finally he succeeded in naturalising two species *p. auricula Linn* and *p. pubescens Jacq:* and of these he sent roots to his friend Van de Delft in Belgium, whence they were spread and during the first half of the seventeenth century they were amongst the most loved of cultivated plants by garden lovers, both on the continent and in England. Indeed the auricula is the only alpine plant which has become an established favourite as a garden flower. When de l'Escluse left Vienna he kept up an active correspondence with Viennese nobles, ladies, apothecaries and others, and there is little doubt that the cult of this beautiful alpine flower owed much to this great botanist's love for it. It is interesting to remember that in this country we owe the introduction of auriculas largely to the Hugenot refugees who brought so many of their favourite flowers with them.

The narcissi which figure so prominently in the *hortus Floridus* had been cultivated in European gardens since about 1500, although some of the species were doubtless grown even in outlying parts of the Roman Empire. *N. pseudo-Narcissus* is described by the most modern authorities as a native British plant. Parkinson in his *Paradisus* calls it "Gerard's double Daffodil" and describes it as "assuredly naturall of our owne Countrey, for Mr. Gerard first discovered it to the world, finding it in a poore womans Garden in the West parts of England, where it grew before the woman came to dwell there, and, as I have heard since, is naturall in the Isle of Wight". [This daffodil is still found wild in the Isle of Wight]. In *hortus Kewensis N. poeticus* is also described as a native of Britain, but Phillips in his *Flora historica* [1824] says of *N. poeticus*—"This Narcissus seldom produces seed in England, even by the assistance of cultivation and we are therefore of opinion that the few plants which have been found at Shorne, between Gravesend and Rochester, as well as those discovered in Norfolk are the offsets from imported plants, probably of as early a date as the time of the Romans, who we may naturally conclude would not fail to plant the flower of their favourite poet, when we discover that they paved the floors of their dwellings with tessellae that represented his tales". Gerard in his Herbal [1596] describes several narcissi popular in Elizabethan times including the double flowered variety of *N. polyanthus* sent from Constantinople "to the Rt. Honourable the Lord Treasurer among other bulbed flowers" whilst Parkinson describes no less than 100 varieties including all those which figure in the *hortus Floridus*. Gerard describes narcissi by the old English names Daffodowndilly, Chalice Flowers and Lent Lilies. "Daffadillies" [used by both Shakespeare and Milton] is probably a corruption of the word Asphodel; "Lent Lilies" doubtless referred to the time at which most of them flowered, whilst the name "Chalice flower" was applied by the older botanists to varieties such as *incomparabilis* of which the corona resembles a chalice. *N. poeticus* is still known in Cheshire by the pretty old name of "Sweet Nancy."

The crown imperial which is shown in the foreground of the spring garden had only been recently introduced, but even in Gerard's time it was already a first favourite. Parkinson says of it "The Crowne Imperiall for his stately beautifulness deserveth the first place in this our Garden of delight" and Gervase Markham describes the Crown Imperial as "of all flowers both forraigne and home-bred, the delicatest and strangest: it hath the true shape of an Emperiall Crowne, and will be of divers colours, according to the art of the Gardner. In the middest of the flower you shall see a round Pearle stand, in proportion, colour, and orientnesie like a true naturall Pearle, onely it is of a soft liquid substance. This Pearle if you shake the flower never so violently will not fall off, neither if you let it continue never so long, will it either encrease or diminish in the bignesse, but remayneth all one: yet if with your finger you take and wipe it away, in lesse then an houre after you shall have another arise in the same place, and of the same bignesse. This Pearle if you taste it upon your tongue, is pleasant and sweet like honey."

The "Spring Garden" which forms the frontispiece of the book is one of the most charming illustrations of gardens of the period which have come down to us. It depicts a formal garden with a pergola in the background, carved rails in the foreground and the beds planted in the sparse fashion characteristic of that time. All the flowers engraved in the subsequent pages are shown in the garden and the lady with the ruff is picking tulips.

ELEANOUR SINCLAIR ROHDE.

HEPATICA
WITH SNOW-WHITE FLOWER.

I
HEPATICA TRIFOLIA
WITH BLUE DOUBLE FLOWER.

As Hepatica trifolia in general has elsewhere been described by us, we will show here in addition two species of it, not common: one abounding in a double deep blue flower, which is also called *Hepatica trifolia caerulea polyanthos*; the flower of which differs from the common form by the great number of petals and is of a deeper blue colour, and according to Clusius grows commonly in certain places in Hungary, but in our own country it is somewhat difficult of cultivation. The flower of the second species agrees with the common one in form but is altogether of a transparent snow-white colour, the depth of which seems to contain something of a red-purple, and in the centre is bedecked with scarlet threads, from which the white anthers hanging like pearls afford quite a pleasing sight.

Lati. Hepatica trifolia cærulæa polyanthos.
Germ. Dubbelen blawen Hepatica.

L. Hepatica trifolia flore niveo.
Ge. Edel Levercruyt met witte bloemen.

CROCUS VERNUS
WITH A SMALLER PURPLE FLOWER.

II CROCUS NEAPOLITANUS
WITH A LARGER PURPLE FLOWER.

The flower of the Crocus, also not unknown in the stories of the poets, into which the youth, inflamed with hopeless love for the maid Smilax, was transformed according to Ovid, as it is written in this verse, li, 4. Metam: *Et Crocum in parvos versum cum Smilace flores.* There are several species: here we illustrate the vernal broadleaved purple Crocus, varying very much in size. The earlier agrees almost with *Crocus silvestris violaceus* of Lobel: its flower emerges from its sheath in the same manner as the others from a short stalk, with six petals of a violet colour tending to purple; although the top of the little stem together with the beginning of the flower approaches a very dark hue. The later called from its place of origin Neapolitanus, puts forth a flower larger, and distinguished by its more pleasing appearance; likewise consisting of six petals, the three inner and shorter of which are encompassed by the outer as with a caressing embrace. In the centre a golden style emerges surrounded by white threads passing into yellow nodules, and diffusing a somewhat pleasant scent.

2

L. *Crocus Neapolitanus flo: purp: major.*
Ge. *Saffraen vanden Lente met gro: purp: bloe:*

L. *Crocus Vernus purpureus minor.*
Ge. *Saffraen vanden Lête met kley: purp: bloe:*

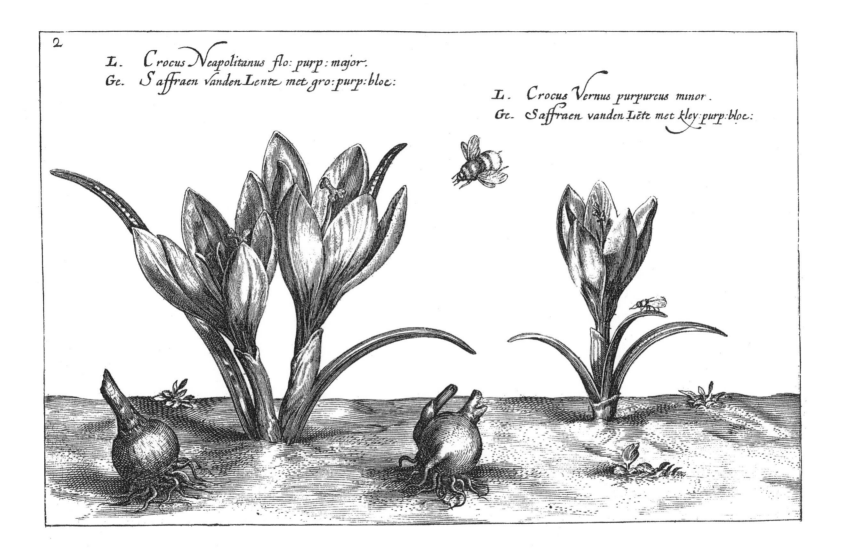

III
YELLOW PSEUDONARCISSUS WITH DOUBLE FLOWER.
PSEUDONARCISSUS WITH DOUBLE FLOWER & TRIPLE TUBE.

The *Pseudonarcissus multiplex* or *pleno flore luteus* [yellow with double flower] puts forth leaves much resembling those of a leek or a true Narcissus: but owing to the great number of its petals it has in the centre of the flower no projecting cup as in the other species. Its colour is deeper round the edges and the root also is bulbous.

The other Narcissus here pourtrayed, of the nature of a monstrosity, produces root and leaves in the same way, and bears a flower remarkable for a triple tube, of golden colour and with fringed edges, in the centre of which projects a solitary style, shorter and not reaching the mouth of the tube: Flowers in the month of April and is rarely found after that time.

L. *Pseudo Narcissus calice ple:multipl:*
colore luteo Dod:
Ge. *Dubbelde geele Tytloosen.*

3

L. *Narcissus duplice tuba flo:lut: Cluf:.*
Ge. *Narc: met die*
dubbel trompet.

The LARGEST NARCISSUS OF ALL.

IIII The LARGEST NARCISSUS, WITH DOUBLED PETALS.

This rare kind of Narcissus, which Christianus Porretus, pharmacist of Leyden in Holland, patron of all the graces, grows in his own garden, and with which is found no other of its kind comparable, or equal in size – whence also it gets its French name: It has leaves a foot-and-a-half tall, gray, rather broad and almost keeled. The two feet long stem bears a single large flower consisting of six pale or faint yellow petals, broad but shortly pointed, surrounding a central yellow tube more than one inch long, narrower in the lower part but more open above, crinkled at the edges: in the middle is a short saffron-yellow style surrounded by six anthers, sprinkled as it were with a yellow meal, rather than by stamens. The scent of the flower is not unpleasing but faint.

The second *Narcissus Maximus* is not very different from the former except that with its doubled petals and more open and sinuous tube it shows itself with greater elegance.

L. *Narciss maxi: dupl: folijs.*
Gc. *Grooten dubb:*
   Narciss.

L. *Narcissus omnium maximus.*
G. *Narcissus nompareille*

MUSCARI
WITH SCENTED YELLOW FLOWER.

MUSCARI
WITH DULL WHITE COLOUR OF DODENS.

Muscari is a kind of false Hyacinth producing long slightly keeled leaves: it sends forth long not very firm stems often more than nine inches tall and from the middle upwards and all round the stem many flowers, small, hollow and of a very pleasant scent recalling somewhat musk [whence also this plant takes its name among the Greeks]: it has a root, like other Hyacinths, bulbous, reddish, and clinging rather deeply and firmly in the earth by somewhat thick fibres [which even last through winter].

Two species are illustrated here, of which the former bears a faintly yellowish flower, while the flower of the latter is whitish and of a dull colour. In other respects with a slight difference they seem almost to agree.

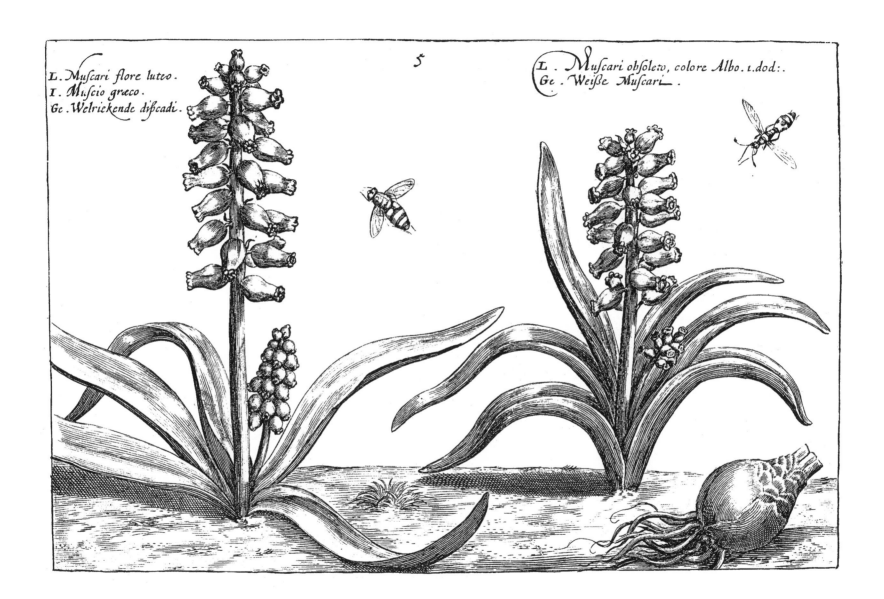

L. Muscari flore luteo.
I. Muscio græco.
Ge. Welriekende discadi.

5

L. Muscari obsoleto, colore Albo. 1. dod:.
Ge. Weiße Muscari.

VI
THE STELLATE HYACINTH OF AQUITANIA WITH BLUE FLOWER.
THE STELLATE HYACINTH OF SPAIN WITH SNOW-WHITE FLOWER.

This stellate Hyacinth with the leaf of a lily is common in the mountains of Aquitania, called by the shepherds Sarahaig, noxious to cattle, is often deadly. It has broad leaves, like the leaves of white lilies, between which comes forth a stem a foot long, quite firm, supporting at intervals several flowers provided with six petals spreading like a star of a violet or deep blue colour. In the centre of these swells up a round disk provided with a circle of filaments: whence appears in triangular pods the seed, black and rather thick, not shining. The bulb does not differ much from the root of Lilium, but is sometimes covered with a distinct cortex with closely crowded bulbils.

The Stellate Hyacinth, with the leaf of Lilium, from Spain, which follows, is almost exactly like the former except that the leaves appear longer and the flower is distinctly snow-white in colour.

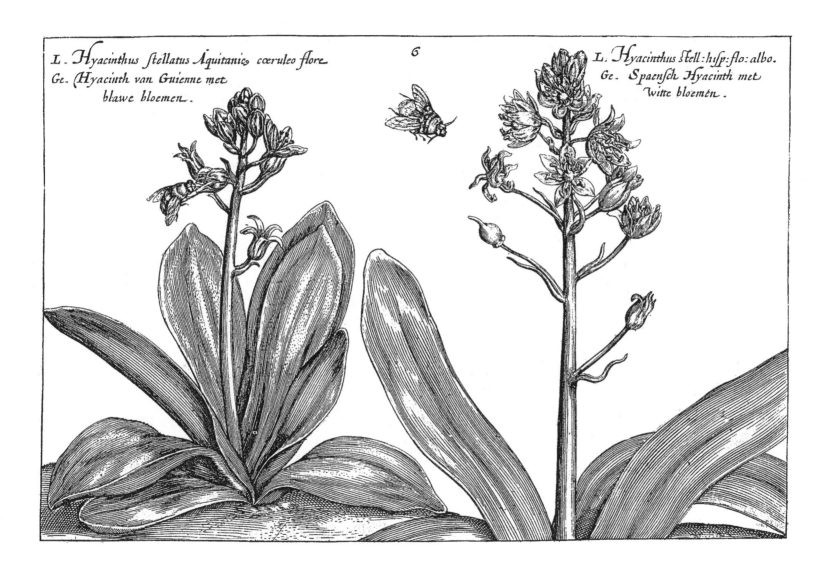

L. *Hyacinthus stellatus Aquitaniæ cœruleo flore.*
Ge. *Hyacinth van Guienne met*
     blawe bloemen.

6

L. *Hyacinthus stell: hisp: flo: albo.*
Ge. *Spaensch Hyacinth met*
     witte bloemen.

VII
PRIMULA VERIS OF BRITAIN WITH DOUBLE FLOWER.

PRIMULA VERIS WITH TWIN FLOWER.

The largest Primula veris of English gardens, with double flower, here pourtrayed, has leaves of a roundish oval, with somewhat crinkled edges, wrinkled with manifold veinlets, resembling Betony, but larger and of a fainter colour, from the centre springs a thin stem, a hand's breadth in height, on the top of which are seen eight, ten or more yellow flowers, remarkable for the great number of petals, with the top of the cup slightly toothed, of the same shape as here illustrated. The root with very many fibres spreads widely and makes it firm in the ground. Very different from the former is the *Primula veris* with a twin flower, one of which grows in the other, similarly of a yellow colour, each like the flowers of *Primula veris*: this plant is now being cultivated with the utmost care in the gardens of Belgium by lovers of Nature's wonders, with its remarkable form not a little delighting the eyes of those who see it. The leaves of the plant are less wrinkled and the stalks from which the flowers hang seem a little thinner and more oblong.

7

L. Primula veris Anglica pleno flore.
I. Fior de primavera.
G. Brayes de Cocu doubl:
Ge. Dubb Schluetel-bloemē.

L. Primula veris flore gemino.

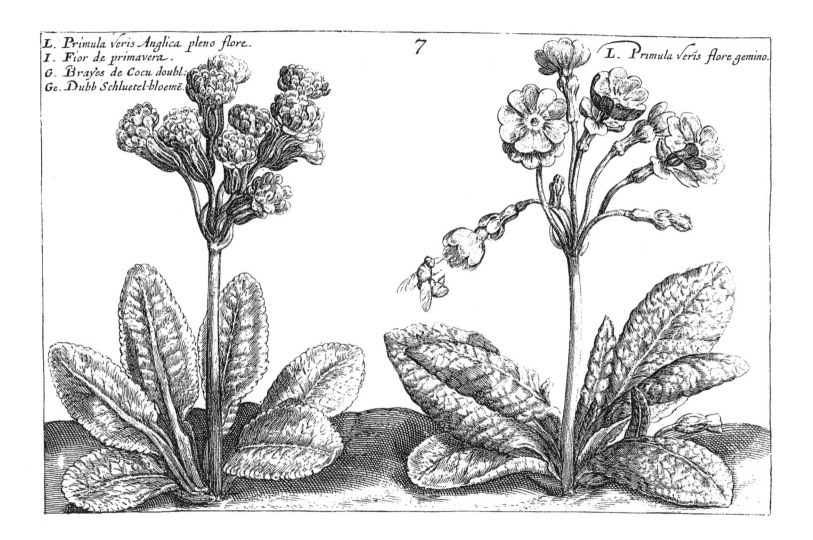

AURICULA URSI
WITH YELLOW FLOWER OF DODOENS.

AURICULA URSI MAJOR
WITH PURPLE FLOWER.

Auricula Ursi seems to be a species of Solidago, and does not differ much in form from *Primula Veris*, having almost similar leaves, but smooth, not wrinkled with veins or nerves, rather thick and sprinkled as it were with meal, and more crinkled at the edges; among the leaves springs a round thin stem from the top of which arise florets each with a little stalk, of a yellow colour but faint and sometimes tending to sulphur-yellow, adorned with five or six incisions in place of petals; having in the centre a white circlet provided with some filaments and sometimes also a small style. The smell is mostly sweet and honey-like. After the flowers comes the seed, unequal in size and black, enclosed in little sacs.

The other species here pourtrayed, has shorter leaves, broader and nearly round except that round about the root they become narrow and are less thick: the stem also is shorter and bears flowers not indeed so numerous but larger, with a deep purple colour and in a measure recalling a ripe mulberry, which however gradually shows a beautiful violet; becoming somewhat pale purple around the centre and approaching rather to whiteness: in scent they are surpassed by the former.

L. Auricola vrsi flo:lut:.
Ge. Geele Beeren oor.

8.

L. Auricola vrsi flore violaceo.
Ge. Beeren ohr violbraun.

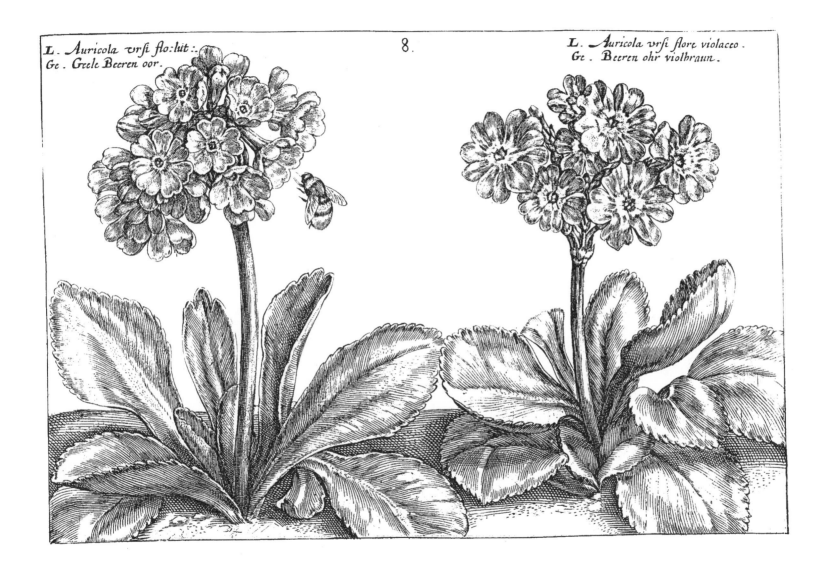

CHAMAEIRIS
WITH VIOLET BLUE FLOWER.

CHAMAEIRIS
WITH DEEP PURPLE FLOWER.

The Chamaeiris here described by us is provided with short broad leaves, and puts forth a flower from a short knotty stem which overtops all the leaves, is broad, and in colour between sky-blue and violet, and marked with darker lines – truly an uncommon spectacle of Nature. It grows in gardens but rarely unless planted. Its roots are jointed, solid, often projecting above the ground, scented, although the flowers are rendered agreeable by no scent.

Subjoined is another species of Chamaeiris, with a flower of a deeper purple colour, resembling somewhat a rough silky purple, and especially bright in the three spreading petals in the middle of which there arises from the lower portion a fringe composed as it were of many slender short yellowish hairs, almost resembling a man's eyebrow: otherwise it does not differ much in shape from other Irises.

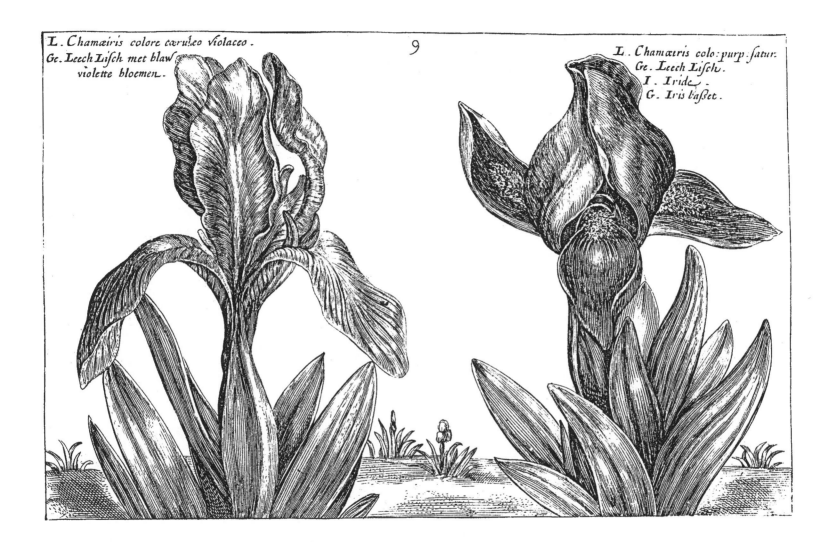

L. Chamæiris colore cæruleo violaceo.
Ge. Leech Lisch met blaw
violette bloemen.

9

L. Chamæiris colo: purp: satur.
Ge. Leech Lisch.
I. Iride.
G. Iris basset.

hyAcINThus ORIENTALIS LATIfOLIUS   hyAcINThus LATIfOLIUS
with BLUE OR PURPLISh FLOWER.   with TWO STEMS & PALE PURPLE FLOWER.

H yacinthus Orientalis, so called because it was originally brought into Italy from the East, is here illustrated ; it has many flowers the colour of which is generally blue, sometimes approaching purple, and sometimes even distinctly snow-white: although they have sprung from the same seed. This Hyacinth has more juicy and broader leaves than the common species, thicker stems and larger more open flowers.

The second and larger Orientalis shows flowers appearing from all round the stem, rarely more than ten in number, of a palish purple colour; it also very often luxuriates with a second stem besides the usual one, to the pleasure of those who see it.

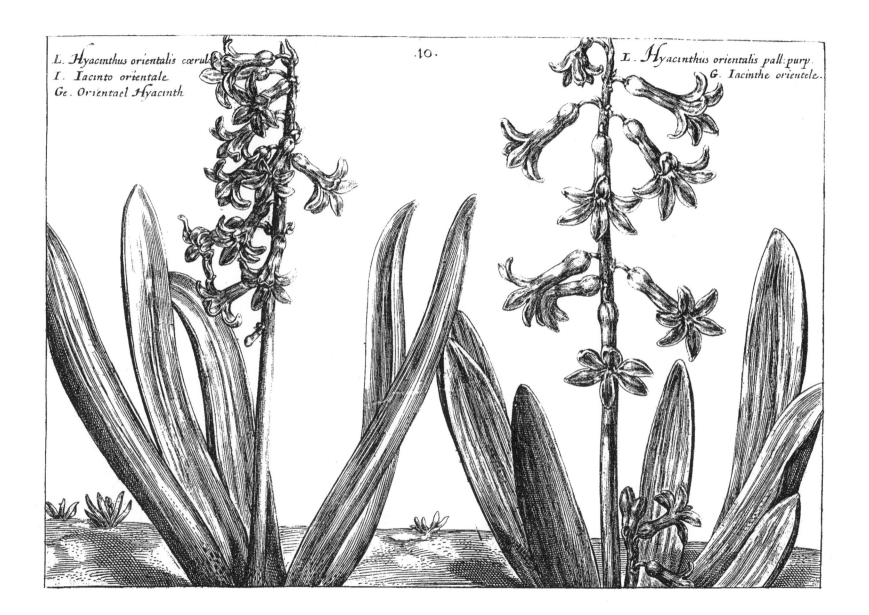

.10.

L. *Hyacinthus orientalis cærul.*
I. *Iacinto orientale*
Ge. *Orientael Hyacinth*

L. *Hyacinthus orientalis pall: purp.*
G. *Iacinthe orientele.*

HYACINTHUS ORIENTALIS XI HYACINTHUS ORIENTALIS
WITH LEAFY STEM.   WITH GREENISH TWIN FLOWER.

Although nearly all the Hyacinths produce a naked stem, there appeared not many years ago the Hyacinth here illustrated, which the very elegant Clusius related that he owed to Mathaeus Caccinus of Florence. Furthermore this has a bulbous root, on a par with the other Asiatic Hyacinths, from which appear five or six leaves, green and keeled, between which arises a nodose stem, nine inches high, surrounded by some leaves closely joined together; the flowers are then unfolded, when the stem takes on its growth, and are observed to surround the stem in no fixed order; on the other hand later and in the month of May fruit appears in pleasing abundance. To the same Caccinus we are indebted for notice of this foreign and rare Hyacinth of Constantinople, likewise first seen a few years ago, the flower of which when it first appears is green, then acquires a bluish colour while it begins to be unfolded; but when opened is white and green, and all its petals retain that green outer nerve occupying the middle of the petals. The stalk bearing the flower is a little longer than in the rest of the Hyacinths. What also adds beauty to the flower, is a second little flower consisting of three petals, bursting from the middle of the flower, which forthwith changes colour like the primary flower; a few stamens occupy the centre of the flower, provided with black anthers.

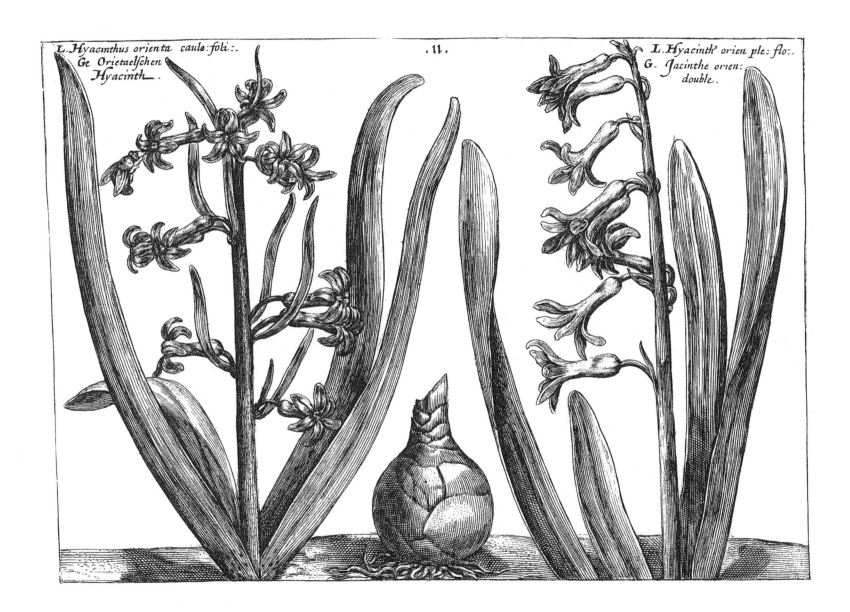

L. Hyacinthus orienta caule: foli:.
Ge Orietaelschen
Hyacinth.

.11.

L. Hyacinth⁹ orien ple: flo:.
G. Jacinthe orien:
double.

XII
CROWN IMPERIAL
WITH A DOUBLE TIER OF FLOWERS.

The Crown Imperial, a plant foreign to us, first sent by Clusius from Constantinople, but Persian in origin, and hence called also by him the Persian lily, belongs to the genus of wild lilies; it has smooth oblong leaves, surrounding the stem in the form of a star as in other wild lilies; and has a stem like to these, except that it is provided on the top with a cluster of several leaves, whence from slender stalks hang the flowers, of six petals, pourtraying in form a lily, but smaller and more closed, and not curved with any flexures; generally of a yellowish colour but sometimes approaching a reddish hue: In the middle of the petals stand forth six little stamens which surround a whitish style. And in place of a root it has a round smooth bulb, not as in the rest of the lilies uneven with crowded bulbils, the smell is unpleasant. Sometimes it grows luxuriantly with several tiers of flowers: And the one which is here figured is remarkable for a double rank of flowers.

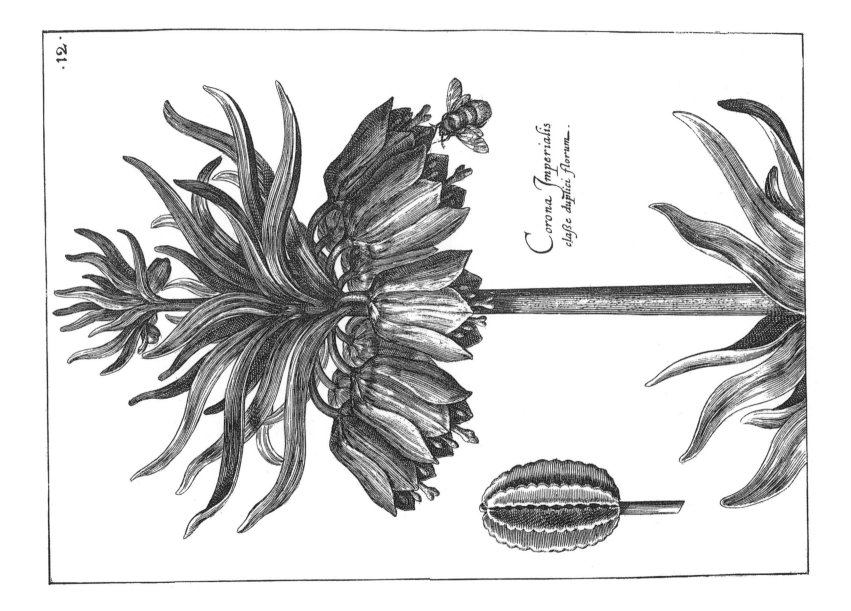

·12·

Corona Imperialis classe duplici florum.

XIII
SLENDER-LEAVED ANEMONE
WITH A SINGLE VIOLET FLOWER.   WITH A SINGLE SCARLET FLOWER
WITH A CRIMSON FLOWER CALLED PRINCEPS.

Anemone, that is wind flower, rightly so called because it never opens except when the wind is blowing, lovely in its wondrous beauty and variety of colours, is wont to delight beyond measure, to attract and as it were to hold the eyes of those who see it. In this place three species of slender-leaved Anemone are figured, distinguished by diversity of colours in the flowers, otherwise with very slight difference. The leaves of the plant are cut, most like the leaves of the wild Ranunculus or Coriander; the root when fairly young resembles a fallen olive, but when old looks like a mass of many spread olives, and appears very much knotted: The flowers spring from slender and downy stalks, and are usually of six petals of a very pleasing aspect in the centre of which are seen the almost purple heads [although these are not always of one colour] surrounded by their stamens and anthers. The first species shows a flower with violet or purple colour; the second purple-red, but the flower of the third species recalls as nearly as possible a crimson silky hairy cloth and on account of its extreme beauty is known as *Anemone princeps*.

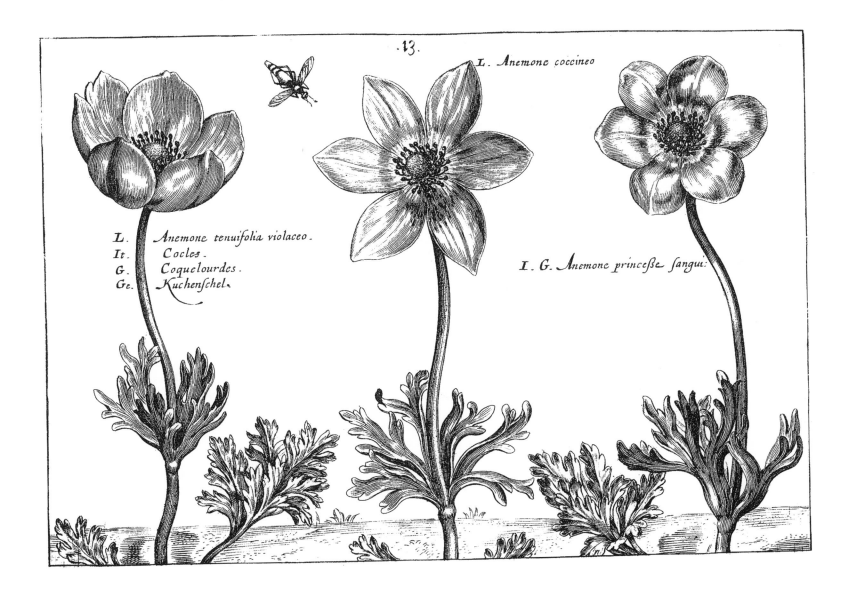

·13·

L. Anemone coccineo

L. Anemone tenuifolia violaceo.
It. Cocles.
G. Coquelourdes.
Ge. Kuchenschel.

I. G. Anemone princeße sangui:

XIIII
SLENDER-LEAVED ANEMONE
THE SECOND KIND OF CACCINUS WITH DOUBLE PALE-RED FLOWER.
BYZANTINE WITH MANY-PETALLED FLOWER.

This former species of Anemone with double flower does not differ much from the Byzantine which follows: The colour of the flower is, in the outer petals that of a fading *Rosa Alabandica*, but the main portion consisting of many smaller petals is a blush-red. The latter, the Byzantine [called lalè by the Turks] has the leaves of *Bulbocastanum*; the flower is remarkable with ten or more broader downy leaves round the circumference, on the outside pale-red but inside resplendent with a deeper colour; a larger and almost endless number of slender smaller petals, of a crimson or even pale purple colour, fill the centre of the flower. The root is knotted and more oblong, not black on the outside but dusky. This plant is sometimes seen to produce flowers a second time in Autumn, but they are less elegant; the central small petals of these flowers maintain a quince-like and greenish colour, due [as I think] to want of warmth, and are as it were crude and immature.

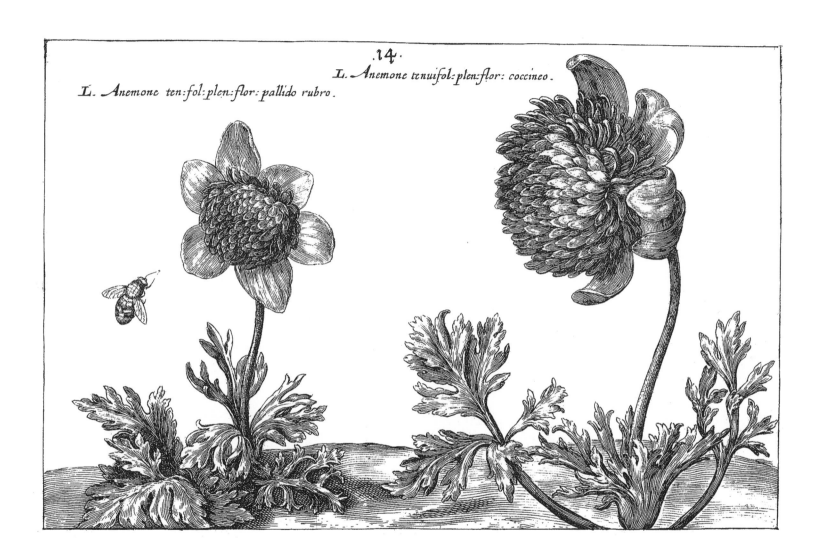

.14.

L. Anemone tenuifol: plen: flor: coccineo.

L. Anemone ten: fol: plen: flor: pallido rubro.

XV
SLENDER-LEAVED ANEMONE
VERDUNIA, WITH SINGLE VIOLET FLOWER. SPANISH, WITH FLOWER FLESH COLOUR. SINGLE WITH ORANGE FLOWER.

In the flowers of the broad-leaved Anemones so great variety of colours is seen that it is very difficult to express in words; the number also of the petals of which they consist varies in a remarkable manner. The leaves of the plant are broader and divided into fewer segments; the root also is tuberous and surrounded by its root-fibres. Three species are figured here; the first, *Verdunia*, commonly so called by a certain grower in Holland, has a flower of seven petals, the colour of which passes into a violet or lanthine from a silver base; the downy head becomes black and is surrounded by white filaments with bluish anthers. The second, *Hispanica*, the flower of which of flesh colour [which is commonly called *incarnatus*] consists of twelve or thirteen petals, forming a circle round the head and stamens: The third has a flower of eight petals, resplendent in a beautiful red and yellow colour [which the Belgians call Orange], the small stamens of which, bedecked with blue anthers, surround the head.

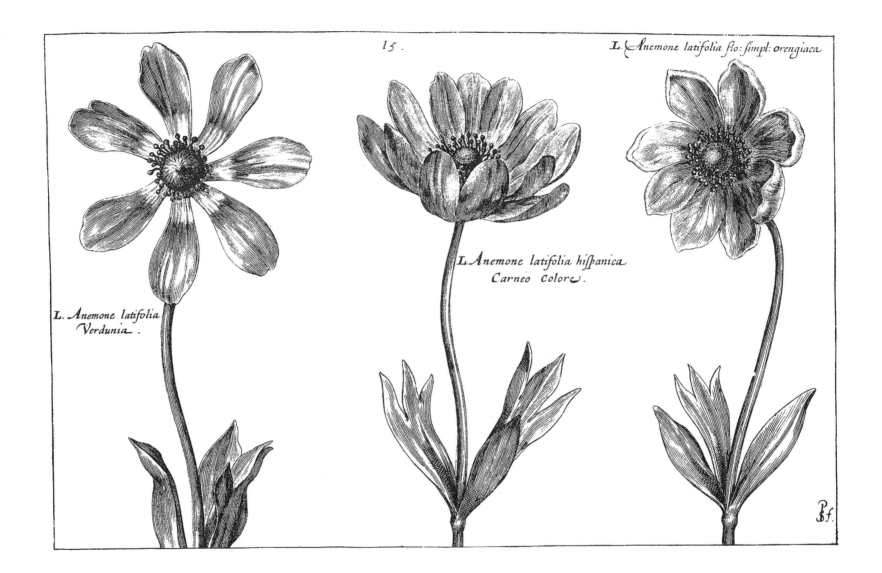

15.

L. Anemone latifolia flo: simpl: orengiaca

L. Anemone latifolia hispanica Carneo Color.

L. Anemone latifolia Verdunia.

Pf.

SLENDER-LEAVED ANEMONE
PAVO [PEACOCK] WITH SINGLE FLOWER.   PAVO MAJOR MULTIPLEX.

The broad-leaved garden Anemone, called *Pavo secunda*, produces a single flower, provided with broader petals passing into a point, seven, eight or more in number of a scarlet colour. The second species of Anemone, bears a flower, with twenty or thirty petals sometimes an inch in length, the colour of which is a rather deep purple-red, with a crimson base passing into a yellowish circlet around the central portion [which is downy, blackish and girt with crimson stamens ending in blue anthers]. The roots of these Anemones are rather thick, knotty, firm, of a dusky colour externally, dead white inside, and surrounded with many slender fibres.

L. *Anemone pavo flore fimplici.*   L. *Anemone pavo Major.*

XVII
BROAD-LEAVED ANEMONE
chALCEDONICA mAxImA mAny FloWered. chALCEDONICA CACumeNI.

This *Chalcedonica maxima* has leaves larger than the other Anemones, harder and provided with several nerves; a broad and spreading flower, of many petals, of which the ten or twelve outer are green, remarkable for a network of scarlet veins, the inner petals are smaller and more slender, brilliant with a somewhat pale purple and soft red colour, about the centre they retain the same colour but appear bent back and somewhat crisped.

The second *Anemone Chalcedonica ex Cacumenis* of which the worthy Mathaeus Caccinus of Florence made mention in his letters, was indeed named by Clusius but not yet fully known, nor at all events described; it is figured here; it bears a flower with a triple series of striking petals, not of one colour only but flame-colour crimson and snow-white, a very pleasing variety of mixture, embellished also with a whitish base, and has instead of stamens certain small narrow erect petals of a yellow-green colour occupying the centre.

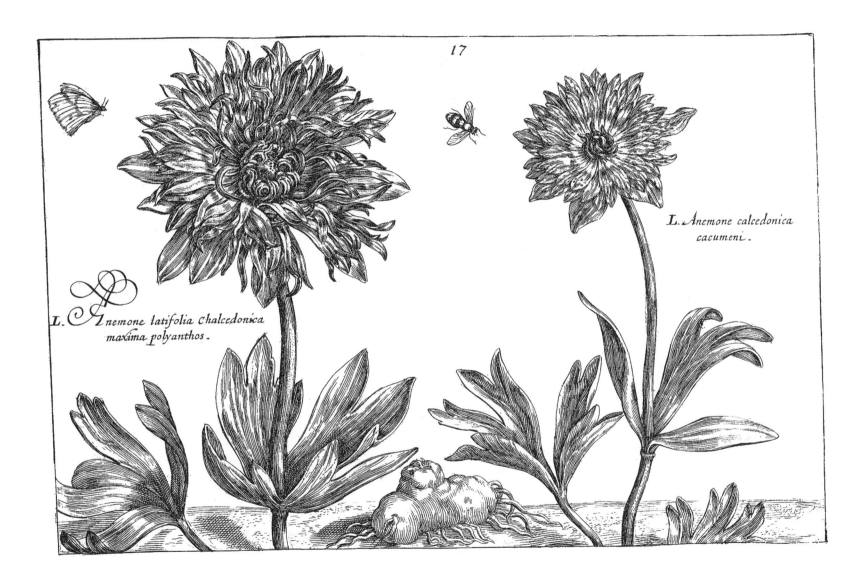

L. *Anemone latifolia Chalcedonica maxima polyanthos.*

L. *Anemone calcedonica cacumeni.*

XVIII
SLENDER-LEAVED ANEMONE
FLOWER OF ADONIS. ERANTHEMUM OF DODOENS. BUPHTHALMUM DODOENS.

The herb, which Dodonaeus calls *Eranthemum*, and Mathiolus wrongly the flower of Adonis, since that flower very well known from the tales of the poets, seems to be a species of Anemone, puts forth from its root several small stems, divided forthwith into branches, sesiated, and green; slender leaves, like those of Chamomile; flowers not large, shaped like the flowers of Ranunculus, beautiful vermilion red in colour; a small oblong head succeeds the flowers, an aggregate of many roundish seeds, coming to a point, of a somewhat dark green colour: roots fibrous.

In the plant to which is given the name *Buphthalmum*, small slender stems arise from the roots, three four or more feet or taller, and around these green leaves with slender segments, like the leaves of fennel, but much smaller; large flowers on the top of the stalks, very like a Marigold, of a golden-yellow colour, with yellow stamens in the centre, and after the flowers follows a small head, as in *Eranthemum* described above, constructed of many seeds joined together: the roots are slender and fibrous, like the roots of the black Veratrum.

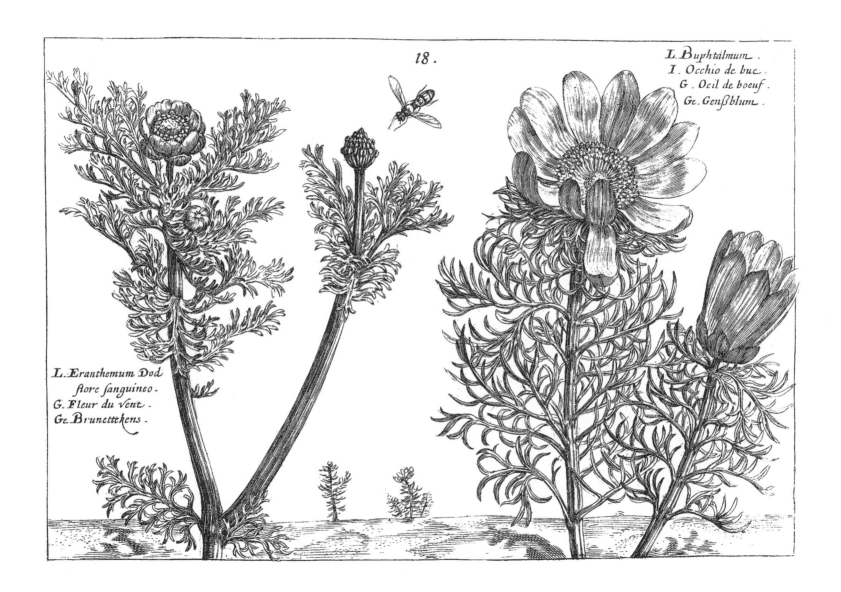

18.

L. Eranthemum Dod
flore sanguineo.
G. Fleur du vent.
Ge. Brunettekens.

L. Buphtalmum.
I. Occhio de bue.
G. Oeil de boeuf.
Ge. Genßblum.

XIX
NARCISSUS TENUIFOL

FLORE ALBO MEDIO PURPUREO, DOD.   FLORE ALBO MEDIO LUTEO, LOB.

The first Narcissus, with a red centre, [also mentioned by Dioscorides] has fresh green oblong leaves resembling those of a leek: a naked somewhat angular stem, more than a foot tall, and at the top a flower bursting from a membrane, generally one only, but sometimes a pair, of moderate size, scented, built up of six glistening-white leaves, in the centre of which is a short circular cup, with red edges, whence it is called *Narcissus purpureus* both by Pliny and Virgil; inside the cup are short stamens with yellowish anthers: the angular fruits appearing later contain black seed; the root is bulbous like an onion and sending out kernels from itself is easily multiplied into many bulbs.

The second Narcissus, described by Lobel as yellow in the centre, has broader and taller leaves, stems also taller and thicker and somewhat flattened, on each of which are three or four flowers similar in shape to the former, except that in this case from one and the same stalk a third flower may appear, larger and with double leaves; the tube is yellow with saffron-coloured crisped edges.

Croceum pro corpore florem
Invenient, foliis medium cingentibur albis.

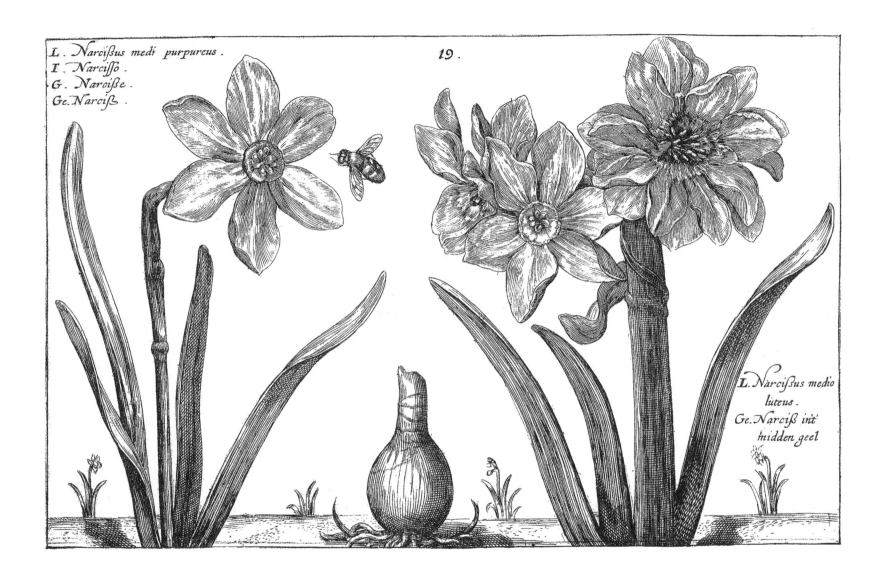

L. Narciſsus medi purpureus.
I. Narciſso.
G. Narciſse.
Ge. Narciß.

19.

L. Narciſsus medio
luteus.
Ge. Narciß int'
midden geel

XX
BROAD-LEAVED NARCISSUS
WITH YELLOW-CENTRED FLOWER AND RATHER OBLONG CUP.

The Narcissus here figured in the first position usually appears in April, and has erect and somewhat keeled leaves, a flower usually solitary, oblong, hanging from a rather tall stalk, the six long shortly pointed glistening white petals of which encircle an oblong tube of a yellow colour with somewhat crinkled margins, having in its centre a rather pale style surrounded by six stamens whose tips seem in a manner to be sprinkled, with a yellow meal. Its scent is not unpleasant.

The second Narcissus differs little from the former, but has broader leaves, keeled deep green and not unlike the leaves of Hyacinths, it bears also generally two flowers springing together from one membranous sheath. So forsooth, does Nature sport with pleasing variety in flowers of the same kind, and, often aided by human assiduity, bids even well known flowers appear masked as it were in unwonted dress.

20

L. *Narcißus oblongo calice.*

L. *Narcißus medius lute*
amplo cal: clusij.

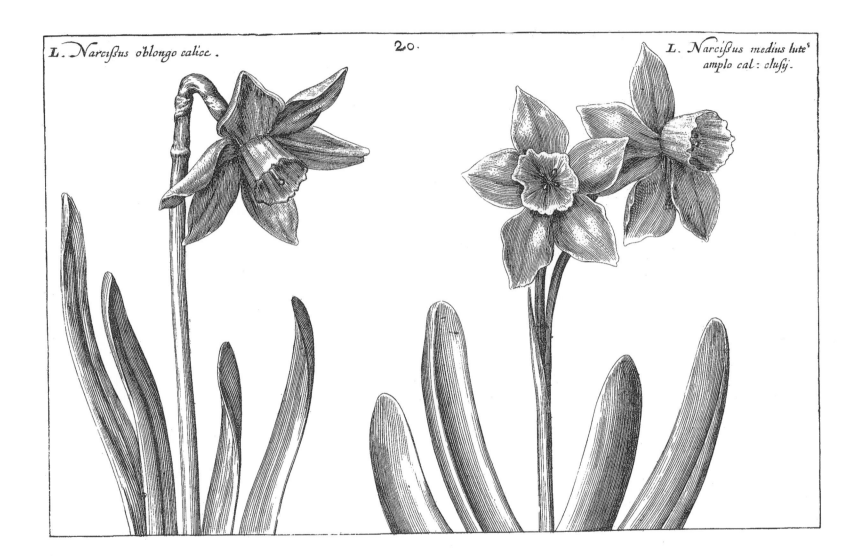

XXI
SLENDER-LEAVED NARCISSUS
WHITE THROUGHOUT THE FLOWER. WITH WHITE SOMEWHAT DOUBLE FLOWER.

A Narcissus with flower white throughout including the centre, is here described; the leaves of which are oblong and less green, the stem indeed bears four or more flowers, not so large as the flowers of the remaining Narcissus, white throughout, with a small and short cup of the same colour. It is found in many places in Spain.

The Narcissus which follows is found nowhere except in gardens, and usually appears later, namely in the month of May, having tall leaves and a stem shorter than the leaves, which bears a rather large flower, with six broad keeled white petals displayed in the form of a star, the centre of which, in place of a cup, six other smaller petals occupy, likewise white but showing somewhat of a yellowish colour scattered here and there; some stamens nevertheless adorn the centre.

21

L. *Narcißus totus albidus*

L. *Narcißus flore multiplici.*

XXII
BROAD-LEAVED NARCISSUS
with palish flower & broad yellow cup. Larger, yellow in the centre.

From a bulbous somewhat oblong root provided with many fibres, this Narcissus puts forth three or four leaves, somewhat broad, a foot and a half long, between which arises a naked stalk, a foot in length, bearing on the extreme summit a single flower, emerging from a membranous sheath, consisting of six pale or pale yellow petals from the centre of which is a cup or rather broad tube, with fringed edges, of a golden colour; in which are six rather short stamens, furnished with yellow anthers, and a central style shorter than the stamens.

The second and larger Narcissus is more common in Italy, and has a stem much longer than the other Narcissi, so that it stands up sometimes as much as three feet; from this hang several flowers from their stalks of a quince or sulphur-yellow, yet not altogether of a dull or rather sad colour, having in the centre a golden tube; of a somewhat sweet smell.

L. Narcissus maximus griseus calice flavo. 22

L. Narcissus maior medio lute' Italicus.

XXIII
RUSH-LEAVED NARCISSUS
FLOWER WITH AN AMPLE YELLOW CUP WITH WHITE REFLEXED FLOWER

The former Narcissus has leaves like the rest of the narrow-leaved Narcissi, and very little different from rushes; and in the midst of them arises a stem slender but strong, a foot in length, on the top of which from a thin sheath three or more flowers arise, elegant, scented, and larger than in the common *juncifolii*, consisting of six small yellow petals in the centre of which is a cup of saffron colour exceptionally broad with margins, as appears, folded; from this cup project six short yellowish stamens embellished with golden anthers, surrounding a style of the same colour which passes into a thicker little knob.

In the case of the second Narcissus also arising from the group of the *juncifolii*, two, three or more flowers spring from a membranous involucre, hanging down, snow-white, oblong, with six petals bent back like a Cyclamen, with a projecting tube the length of an inch with uneven margins, in which three small white stamens embellished with yellowish anthers surround a central style which overtops them; and succeeding this are trigonous heads laden with roundish black shining seed. It is of common occurrence in the Pyrenean mountains.

23

L: *Narcissus Iuncifolius amplo cal:lut:.*   **L.** *Narcissus Iuncifolius albo flore reflexo.*

RUSH-LEAVED NARCISSUS

WITH DOUBLE FLOWER.   FLOWER WITH A VERY LARGE CUP.

From a bulbous root, this very rare plant puts forth four or five erect, smooth, narrow green leaves, among which rises up an erect stem, without a node, green and quite strong, supporting right at the top a membranous sheath, like the rest of the Narcissi, from which sometimes several flowers spring forth clinging to a somewhat oblong slender stalk and consisting of a multiplex structure of petals; the colour of these flowers is quite golden and the shape altogether different from the common shape of the flowers, in that they lack that longer tube and spring in a cluster directly from the end of the stalk, as also one can see in the double flower of *Anemone latifolia*, in truth a fine sight. It is supposed to bear no seed, since it lacks that swelling which is seen beneath the flower in the common species, but Clusius thinks that propagation is effected by offsets, whence also its greater rarity and its very high estimation by those who possess this plant.

The second and larger Narcissus also of the *juncifolii* kind, produces quite large flowers from one sheath, provided with a very large yellow tube, more spreading round the crinkled edges; in other respects it seems to agree with other narrow-leaved Narcissi.

24

L. *Narcissus Iuncifolius flore pleno.*

L. *Narcissus maximo cal flo: lut.*

XXV
PERSIAN LILY.

This Persian or Susian lily is certainly to be set down among exotic and foreign plants, nor is it very common but only found in the better cultivated gardens; it was kept by Dodonaeus among the False Hyacinths; it puts forth oblong greenish leaves less broad than the leaves of the other lilies, occupying the lower portion of the stem, and this straight round stem rises up to three four or more feet in height, and its upper portion is clad and embellished with a large number of flowers hanging from stalks now longer now shorter. The flowers, consisting of five or six small petals recall the shape of a little pendulous bell and represent most nearly the colour of dark violet, sometimes however approaching more to purple: they open not together but gradually and in a definite order, beginning, namely, below; they are quite lacking in scent. The root consists of a large bulb, in one part round, in another part flat, clinging to the ground by yellowish fibres at the basal portion.

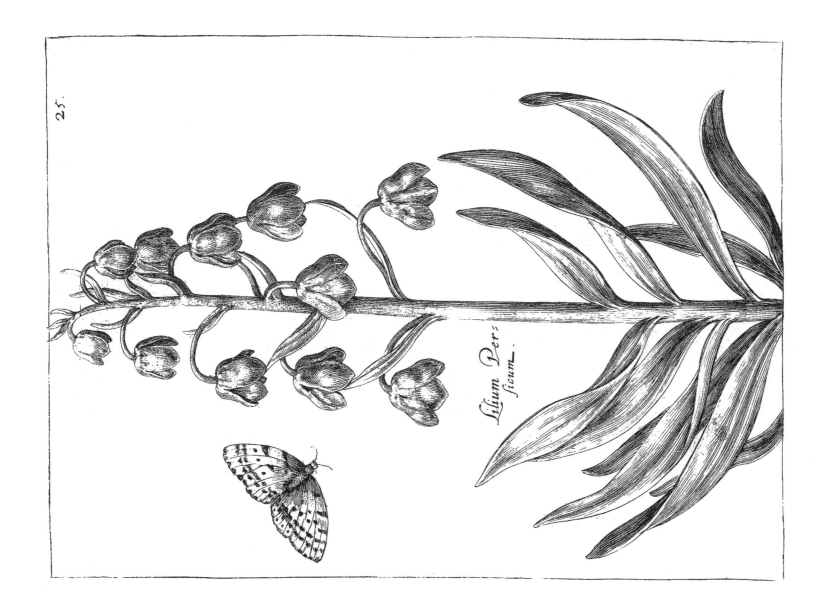

25.

*Lilium Per=
sicum.*

XXVI
EARLY BROAD-LEAVED TULIP
WITH PURPLE FLOWER.   WITH WHITE FLOWER.
WITH REDDISH PURPLE FLOWER, WITH WHITE EDGES.

The Tulip also belongs to the bulbous flowers, a foreign flower, of which there are different species showing the most abundant variety of colours. All the larger have nearly the same form; two or three thick oblong broad leaves becoming slightly reflexed along the edges, and when they first burst forth appear slightly red but when fully grown become white: the stem comes out between them a foot or a little more in height; upon it sits a solitary flower looking upwards, of six petals, resembling somewhat an open rather deep cup with a slightly contracted mouth or a cap of this shape turned upside down.

The cartilaginous flat seed is borne in heads, which when the seed is ripe split into three parts The root is bulbous, but little different from the bulbs of Narcissus. Here three flowers are figured different in their colours; of which the first is arrayed in a purple violet colour not however uniform but with much variety; the second, the most impatient of them all of cold, is white, although sometimes it is bedecked with rosy or purple lines or intermingling veins: the third is almost of a purple-red colour, tending somewhat to purple, remarkable by its whitish claws and margins, as we have lately seen with the greatest delight in the highly cultivated garden of Wolfwinckel.

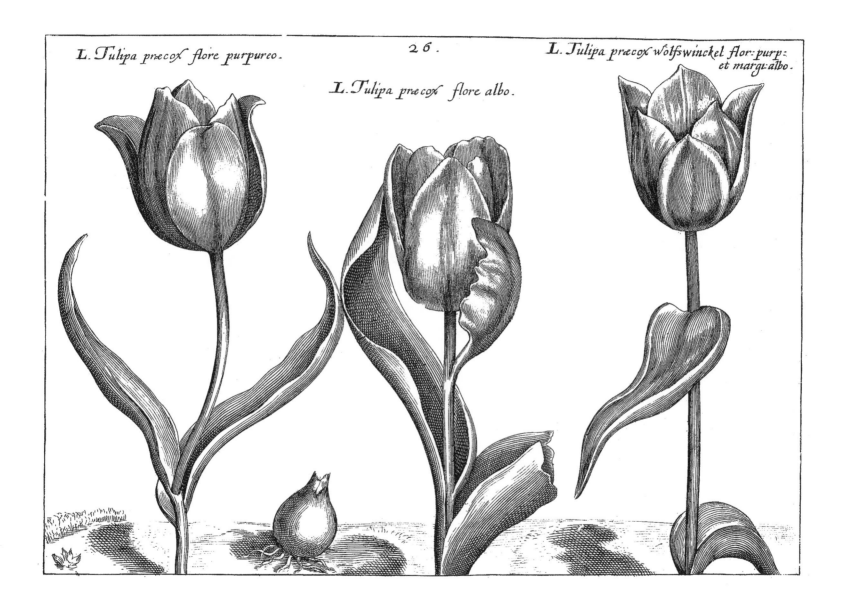

L. Tulipa præcox flore purpureo.

26.

L. Tulipa præcox flore albo.

L. Tulipa præcox wolfswinckel flor: purp: et margi: albo.

TULIP

EARLY PERSIAN.
CRETAN WITH LILY-LIKE LEAF.

The plant of *Tulipa Persica* sent by the illustrious Caccinus to the famous Clusius flowered along with the early Tulips; and put forth in the year 1607 a stem a foot long, quite slender, provided with four leaves, not very broad, in fact not exceeding the breadth of the leaves of the Narbonne Tulip, not so green however but more approaching the colour of the early Tulips, and keeled: and this stem bore right at the top a delicate flower, a little larger than the flower of the Spanish Tulip, consisting of six petals two inches long, three of which are rather long and with a sharp point, outside of a soft reddish colour, yet white on the edges, but inside completely white: the three inner petals which are a little shorter, had the point somewhat rounded, and were completely of a snow-white colour: nevertheless the claws of all were marked with a purple spot: stamens black, anthers also black: Skin of the bulb blackish and dusky outside, filled in the inside with a soft wool somewhat rusty in colour. The petals of our flower of this are nearly all sharp-pointed and seem to differ but little among themselves in form.

The second, first brought from Crete as is believed, hence its name; is provided with leaves broader than of a lily, and bears also an open flower, in the shape of a lily, with a very elegant mixture of white and purple colour, also remarkable for a saffron-yellow base and black stamens, a not unpleasing spectacle.

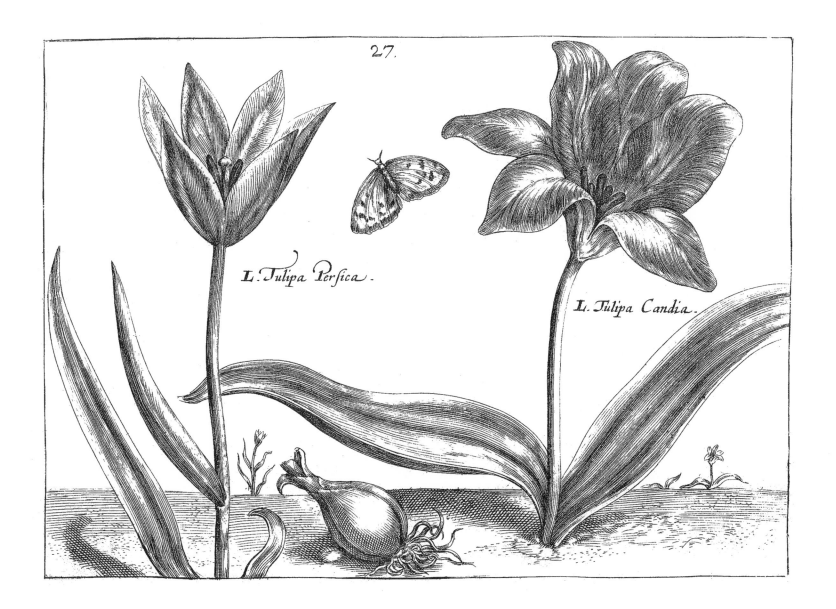

L. Tulipa Persica.

L. Tulipa Candia.

XXVIII
SLENDER-LEAVED TULIP

DWARF.   NARBONENSIS.

The dwarf Tulip, is the smallest of those which are provided with narrower leaves, known to few, and by no-one, so far as I know, hitherto described, except that the appendix of Dodonaeus merely made mention of a dwarf Tulip; the little flower is adorned with a somewhat yellowish colour, decorated besides with ruddy bands and with vermilion veinlets and claws, but in its shape it does not differ much from the *Narbonensis*.

A second is added called *Narbonensis* or *Bononiensis*, which is also named *Appenina* by Clusius; this puts forth a stem more than a foot and a half tall, sometimes divided into several branchlets, from each of which arises a somewhat open flower of a yellow and gold colour, the petals of which are fairly broad and become green outside especially about the base; from the centre of the flower proceeds a rather long three-angled head, surrounded by several yellow stamens; a not unpleasing scent comes from it, almost like that from the yellow Leucojum. The root is bulbous, its bulbil is of the colour of a sweet chestnut, by which it is easily multiplied into several bulbs.

28.

1. *Tulipa Bononiensis*
G. *Tulipa de Montpeliers.*

Tulipa pumilus.

XXIX
BROAD-LEAVED TULIP
DUCALIS, WITH SAFFRON CRIMSON FLOWER. EARLY WITH YELLOW FLOWER. WITH WHITE FLOWER WITH EDGES OF FLESH COLOUR.

Of the broad-leaved Tulips three species remarkable in the difference of their colours, are figured here; the flower of the first of these, one of those commonly called "ducal", is of a very sweet scent, distinguished by a crimson colour in the centre of the petals, with the edges or margins saffron-colour, truly a beautiful sight: the more oblong flower of the second is of a fine yellow colour, and belongs to the early group; while the flower of the third is of a very ample form, white in colour, variegated with pink and purple lines intermingling around the margins.

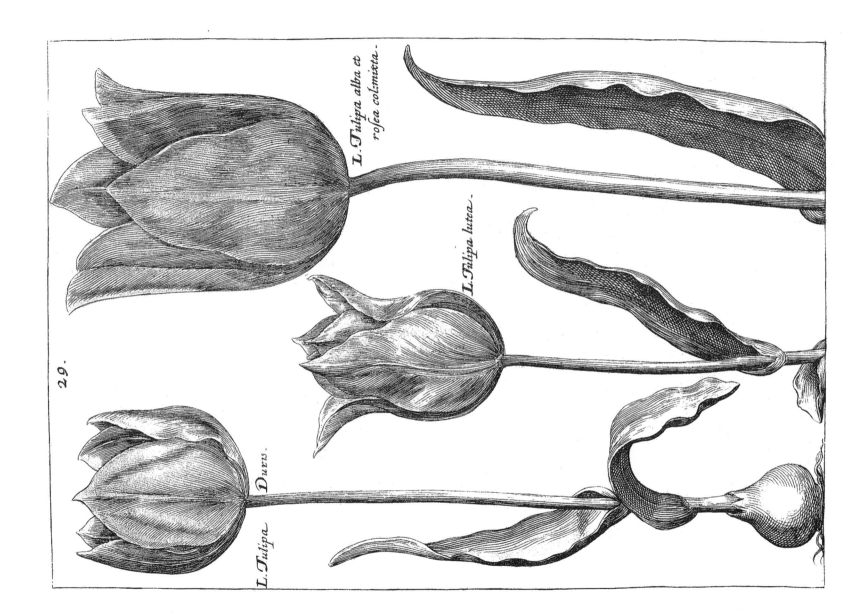

29.

L. Tulipa alba et
rosea colmixtta.

L. Tulipa lutea.

L. Tulipa
Duris.

L. Tulipa

XXX
BROAD-LEAVED TULIP
WITH CRIMSON FLOWER, WITH SCARLET FLOWER VARIEGATED WITH GLISTENING WHITE FLAMES.

The former Tulip, one of the broad-leaved plants, is remarkable for its large flower, of a uniformly brilliant crimson colour, finely embellished with more deeply coloured nerves and veins; the next Tulip flower, lately raised in the garden of Michael Semmius, is more oblong, with a scarlet colour here and there round the edges, tastefully and variously splashed along the centre with glistening white flames, a wonderful marvel of nature.

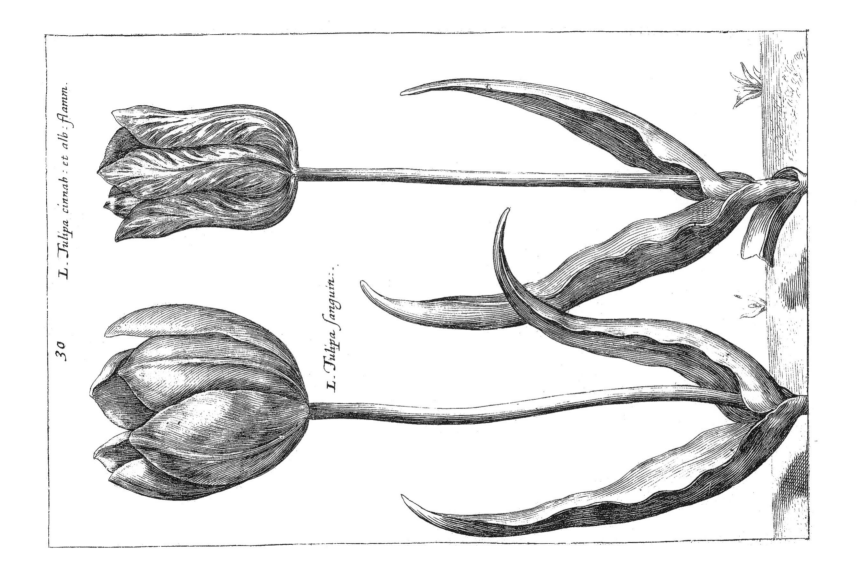

30   L. Tulipa cinnab: et alb: flamm.

L. Tulipa sanguin:

XXXI
BROAD LEAVED TULIP
WITH FLOWER OF ELEGANTLY MARKED SCARLET AND WHITE COLOUR. WITH WHITE CRENULATED FLOWER, WITH SCARLET FLAMES. WITH WHITE FLOWER VARIEGATED WITH SCARLET LINES AND FLAMES.

This first flower of Tulip, known in Holland by lovers of flowers by the name *honestus*, after its grower, by whose care especially it has reached so great excellence of appearance, is wonderful from its silver colour, with varying, now narrower now broader, lines running through it and indefinite spots of scarlet colour, at times also with something of yellow, especially around the base. The one that follows is a very elegant flower, in size indeed yielding to the former, but worthy of no less admiration, for each of its white petals is marked in the middle line from top to bottom by a broad band of scarlet colour, and variegated on each side with smaller flames; the margins are somewhat crinkled or lightly cut. In the last position is placed a more open flower, remarkable with scarlet and white colour promiscuously intermixed in lines, with flames running between, and with a yellowish style.

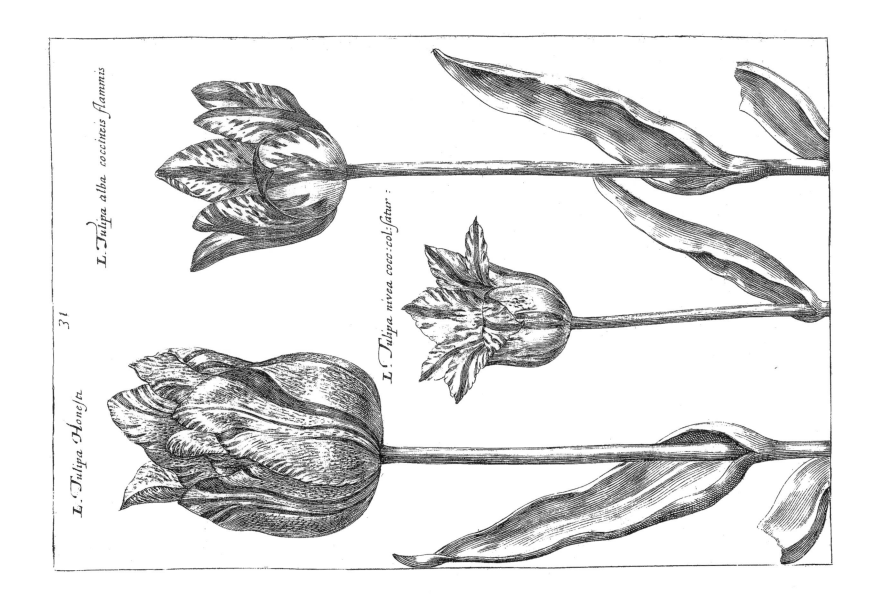

L. Tulipa alba coccineis flammis

31

L. Tulipa Honesta

L. Tulipa nivea cocc::col:fatur:

XXXII
BROAD-LEAVED TULIP CALLED PALTON
WITH A WHITE FLOWER DECORATED WITH A SULPHUR-YELLOW SCARLET COLOUR. WITH A WHITE FLOWER DECORATED WITH RED PURPLE, SULPHUR COLOUR AT BASE.

So great is the variety of Tulips year by year as very often to mock or surpass the desires of the growers, and so it is very difficult even for one who is expert to express them in words.

But this first Tulip can rightly be called *flammea*, its whole flower is resplendent, decorated with flames of sulphur-yellow and scarlet colour: although at the base it is scarcely yellow, at the tops of the petals it is brilliant with flames of a deep purple colour. The flower of the second indeed by no means yields to its companion in elegance, it is less yellow but stands out more brightly with rays of a whitish colour and observers reluctantly withdraw their eyes from it.

32.

L. Tulipa alba cum rubr: flam: et fun: lut:

Willem Pigß:F:

XXXIII
FRITILLARY

WITH PURE WHITE FLOWER.   WITH PURPLE-CHEQUERED FLOWER.

This plant is also called *Meleagris* from the guinea-fowl, the feathers of which its flower resembles; and *Narcissus Caperonius* from its discoverer; it seems to belong to the lilies.

The former has a stem a foot long and sometimes longer, round, slender yet firm, hollow, greenish purple in colour but rather dark; six or more leaves encompass the stem in irregular succession, short, narrow, somewhat keeled; right at the top it bears a pair of flowers, nodding or pendulous like a little bell or tinkler; each of these consists of six petals, straight, of a white colour, becoming slightly yellowish-green about the point; from the centre of the flower appear six white stamens, furnished with yellow anthers, and a central style likewise white, longer, and three-forked at the top; there is no scent.

The flower of the latter is purple, decorated outside with rather pale spots very elegantly and handsomely arranged, on the inside moreover no less pleasing with dark streaks and closely intermingling thin lines; in the centre of the flower rise six small yellowish stamens, with a style of the same colour. The root consists of a bulb like that of a leek, somewhat round and white.

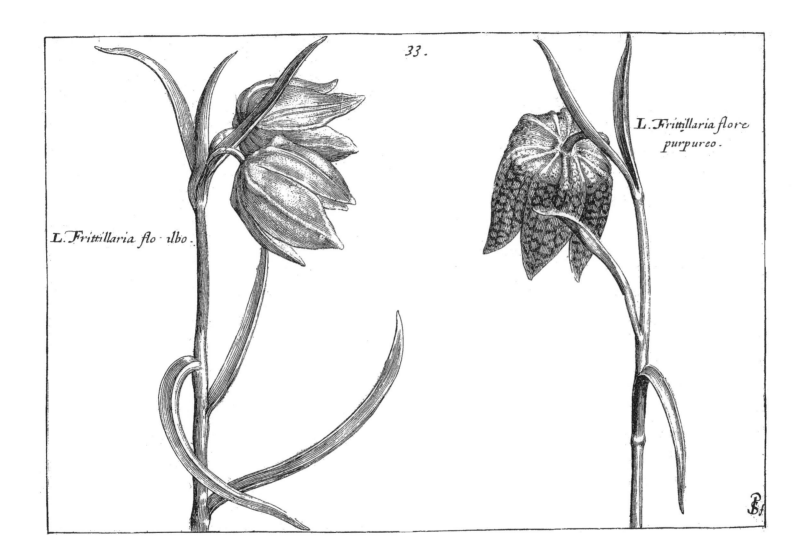

33.

L. Frittillaria flore purpureo.

L. Frittillaria flo· ·lbo.

XXXIIII
FRITILLARY
WITH YELLOW FLOWER MARKED WITH CRIMSON SPOTS. VERY LARGE, WITH MANY PURPLE FLOWERS.

The first Fritillary figured here, bears a flower truly remarkable for a pleasing mixture of colours and spots; the petals of which, gold strewn with elegant crimson spots, distinct, but closely arranged, to a wonderful degree hold the eyes of observers; and they have besides externally greenish nerves standing out along the middle line, adding also their charm to the flower.

The second, which follows, called *Fritillaria maxima*, is very productive in the number of its flowers; and does not lack beauty of its own, since the purple colour in the individual flowers, seems to pourtray a network, now with a pleasing depth, now with a very pale diversity of colour.

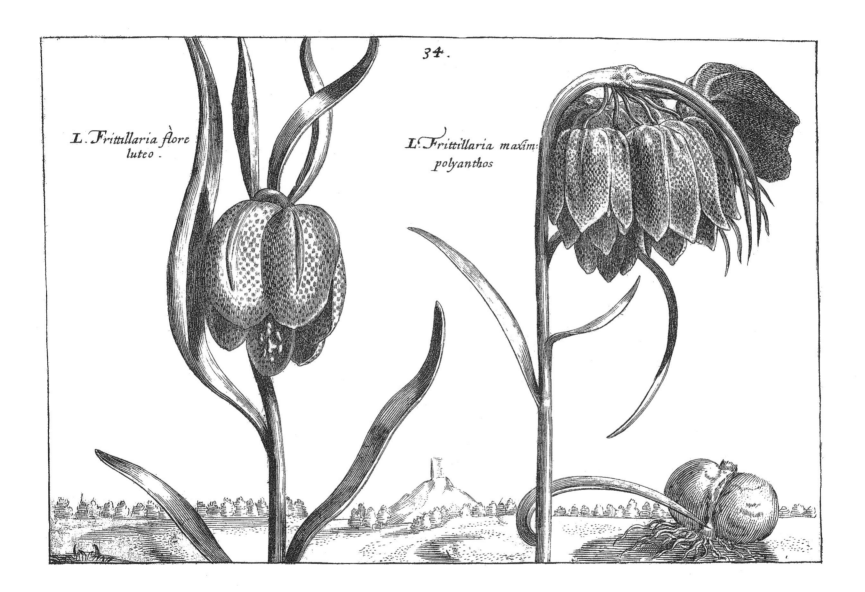

34.

L. Frittillaria flore luteo.

L. Frittillaria maxim: polyanthos

XXXV
ORNITHOGALUM

LESSER.   GREATER

The white flowered bulb [so also Ornithogalum is called] has many leaves and narrow, smaller than those of a grass, the stem comes out between these less than nine inches, round smooth and leaf-less; in the upper part six or seven flowers spring forth distributed on branchlets, outside of an herbaceous green, inside white, constructed of six small petals, and like small lilies especially before they are open; which indeed when the sun is shining spread, but at night and when the air is cloudy, even during the day, remain closed: there follow three-angled heads in which is the small seed: the root is bulbous, full of sticky juice. Two species of it are figured here, differing in size; the first, already described, is smaller, the second, the greater Ornithogalum, is also called the Alexandrine lily, and has everything, namely leaves, stem, flowers, bulb, larger, but is otherwise almost the same.

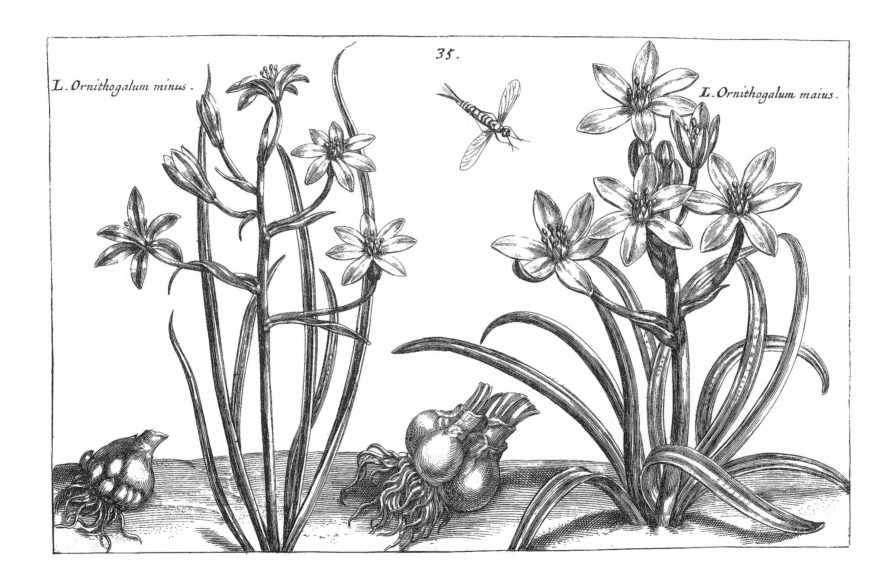

L. *Ornithogalum minus*.

35.

L. *Ornithogalum maius*.

XXXVI
Asphodel

GREATER WITH WHITE FLOWER.   WITH YELLOW FLOWER

The first kind of Asphodel, also called royal spear, has several leaves, rather long, narrow, like the leaves of a leek, passing into a point; a smooth round stem, more than a cubit long; which many spreading flowers of five or six small petals adorn from the middle upwards, in colour white, or becoming slightly purple from a very pale red, with stamens in the centre; after the flowers follow the rounded heads: the seed in this is hard three-angled and of a dull blackish colour; several roots arise from one stock, oblong, thicker below, something like large nuts. In French Provence, Italy and Spain it grows wild: in Germany and Belgium it occurs only when sown.

On the other hand the yellow Asphodel has rather long leaves, furrowed, of a bluish green, longer and narrower than those of the first: stem round, a cubit in length: flowers upon it from the middle upwards also very many, much like those of the other but yellow in colour: roots similarly several, but much more slender and longer than those of the first, yellowish in colour; above the roots certain lateral fibres arise, by means of which the plant itself is multiplied into several others.

I. Asphodelus luteus.

I. Asphodelus albus maior.

36.

AQUILINA   AQUILEGIA
WITH DOUBLE ROSE FLOWER OF A PURPLE COLOUR. WITH STELLATE PURPLE FLOWER.

Aquilegia bears the leaves of the Greater Celandine, but a little more rotund, with cut edge, bluish green in colour, and dry, stem a cubit in length, slender, ruddy, and moderately rough, the branches of which bring forth solitary flowers, formed by the union of many small petals hanging down, hollow like little horns, and as many intermediate raised upwards; in shape pourtraying in a manner a many-petalled rose, in colour of a rich red purple; with stamens bursting forth from the centre, from which hang small anthers: after that the small, black shining seed is produced in several joined pods: the roots are beneath, thick, fibrous, and last several years.

The other species of Aquilegia, produces flowers a little larger, starlike, remarkable also for many series of petals, and purple; for the rest almost like the former.

L. *Aquilina rosea flo:.*
G. *Ancoiles .*

L. *Aquilegia flo:stell:.*
Go *Akeleyen .*

XXXVIII
ASIATIC RANUNCULUS
WITH SIMPLE CRIMSON FLOWER, WITH A TWIN DOUBLE CRIMSON FLOWER.

Batrachium is called in Latin *Ranunculus*, because it delights in places and brinks which are perchance damp. But here two *Asiatic Ranunculi* are figured, the one with a simple, the other with a twin double flower; having at the base three or four leaves, supported by long stalks, cut along the edges, and divided into three segments, rather pale green: between these springs forth the stem quite strong, provided with leaves which are divided into thinner and more numerous segments; on the top of the stalk of the first species a fairly large flower is seated, consisting of six or more petals in a single series, coming in contact with each other at the rounded apex, of a crimson colour throughout, but on the outside rather deeply, on the inside more brightly reddish; the centre of the flower is filled by a rather large and dark head: the root is increased by knobby offsets, whence also bulbils grow and are believed to supply the place of seed.

The double flower of the second *Ranunculus* of the same colour, is so remarkable with its multiplicity of petals, that it is found far to exceed the hundredth number of petals, and what is surprising, puts forth from the centre of the flower another thin stalk which is fruitful with a similar but smaller floret.

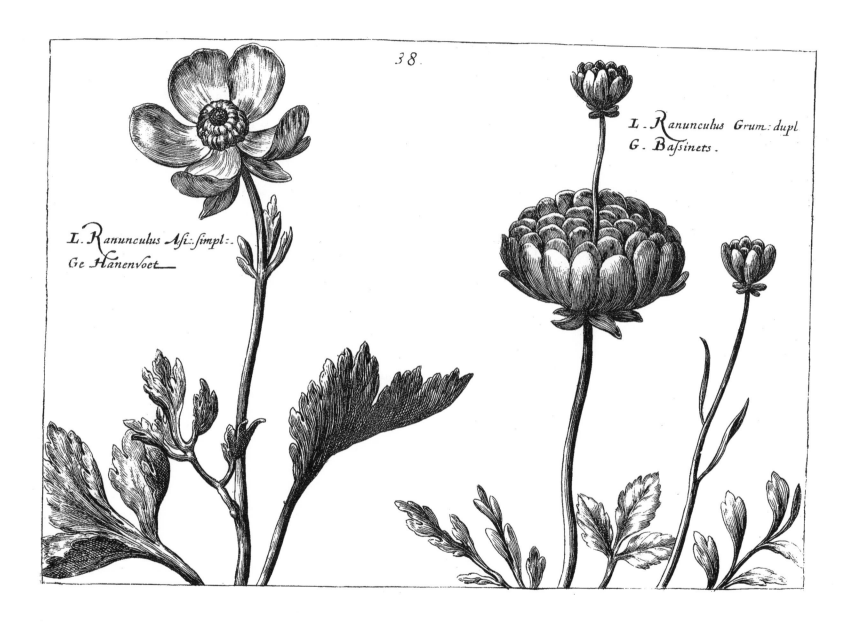

38

L . Ranunculus Grum: dupl
G . Bassinets .

L . Ranunculus Asi: simpl:.
Ge Hanenvoet

XXXIX
RANUNCULUS
GREATER, WITH DOUBLE WHITE FLOWER. GREATEST, WITH YELLOW GLOBOSE FLOWER.

The white double *Ranunculus*, or called from the flower, snow-white many—flowered, is common in the gardens of Belgium, little different from other *Ranunculi*, very like, moreover, the fourth mountain species, except that it seems to excel in size and elegance of flowers.

The second *Ranunculus*, which is called *Maximus* because it far surpasses the others in size, by Gesner also the *Trollius* flower, seems to some to be a species of Aconite because it bears black seed in some pods which are joined together; this however is not approved by Dodonaeus who thinks it ought to be kept among the *Ranunculi*. Its flowers are golden, larger than the other flowers of *Ranunculus*, globular, and consisting of several leaves crowded together and half-closed like a cabbage with a head; the flowers never completely open.

39

I. *Ranunculus albus flore pleno.*

I. *Ranuculus flore globoso maxi:.*

XL
SATYRIUM BASILICON

MALE.

FEMALE.

The larger Satyrium basilicon, which they call male, has broad smooth oblong leaves, smaller than the leaves of a lily, sprinkled with few and hardly visible spots: stems a foot or more high, with leaves growing on them, and at the top white flowers, in a spike, marked with small purple dots, the shape of the testicle of a male Mandrake, except that they lack the crest. Beneath the flowers are born single small leaves running to a point: the twin roots are like hands, each divided into four fingers; one of which is more flaccid and as it were spongy, the other vigorous and firm; a few fibres spring from the place of union.

The other larger sort which they call female, smaller than the former, puts forth leaves of the same shape, but smaller, and shewn with many black spots: flowers like hoods, crested and gaping, like the testicle of Mandrake; in colour scarlet to reddish, variegated with dark purplish narrow lines and dots.

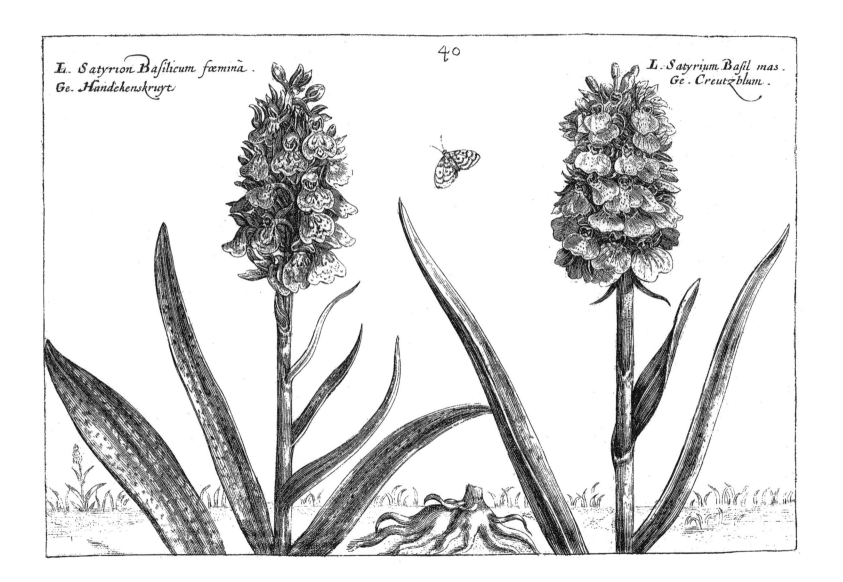

L. Satyrion Basilicum fœminà.
Ge. Handekenskruyt.

40

L. Satyrium Basil mas.
Ge. Creutzblum.

RUSH LEAVED NARCISSUS
XLI
GREATER.   Less.

The larger *Narcissus juncifolius* [the Spaniards call it Jonquillas from the resemblance which the leaves bear to rushes] has narrow rather long leaves, thick, sometimes nearly round in section, quite smooth, and pliant, not very different from rushes; between them springs a stem, on the top of which are three or more small scented flowers, similar in form to Narcissi but smaller and yellow in colour throughout the flower: the bulbous white root is covered by a thin skin. It grows wild in many places in Spain. In Belgium it puts forth flower in the month of April; even in March if the winter has been mild.

The smaller *Juncifolius* is in almost all respects like the larger, except that it is smaller, and has leaves rounder in section and more numerous; it also bears fewer flowers and rarely more than one hanging from one stalk.

L. Narcißus Iuncifol: maior.

41

L. Narcißus Iuncifol: minor.

Rembertus Dodonæus

Carolus Clusius

HORTUS FLORIDUS

BY

CRISPIN DE PASS

HORTUS FLORIDUS

THE SECOND BOOK:

Contayning a very lively and true Description of the Flowers of the

Summer, Autumn and Winter: By

CRISPIN VAN DE PASS:

With a preface by ELEANOUR SINCLAIR RONDE: Calligraphy by MARGARET SHIPTON:

The text translated from the Latin by SPENCER SAVAGE.

PREFACE.

The series of beautiful flower engravings in the "Summer garden" and the "Winter garden" of the *hortus floridus* include the oldest favourites in the garden world. The first engraving depicts a peony, one of the oldest cultivated flowers both in Europe and the Far East. Few flowers indeed can boast of such an ancient genealogy. For over a thousand years the herbaceous peony has been valued in China, not only for its beauty but also for its medicinal virtues. Its name in Chinese signifies "most beautiful" and to this day the fourth moon of the year is "peony moon". In China peonies were the hobby of the wealthy and the finest peony plants until recently so carefully tended in the temple gardens of Peking were said to be 200 years old. The peony figures largely in Japanese poetry and folk-lore, for as early as the eighth century the Japanese had imported tree and herbaceous peonies from China. In the west, according to classical tradition, the peony derives its name from Paeon, a pupil of Aesculapius to whom this flower was given and its merits made known by Leto on Mount Olympus. In gratitude for the marvellous cure wrought by Paeon by means of this flower Pluto changed the physician into the plant which bears his name. It is interesting to recall that we still speak of a "paean" of praise. The earliest description of a peony is to be found in Pliny who describes the plant as "the most ancient of all" and mentions twenty diseases which it cures.

The herbaceous peony was well known to our Saxon ancestors and throughout the Middle Ages it was highly valued not only for its medicinal p operties but the seeds were carried as a protection against witchcraft. In Langland's Vision of Piers Plowman we find that the peony was even used for flavourings. In the fourteenth century poem, "The Pearl", peonies are mentioned as growing amongst the carnations and other flowers near the arbour.

"I entered in that arber grene
In augeoste in high seysoun

. . . .

Shadowed this wortes ful schyre and schere
Gilofre, gingure and groomylyon,
And pyonys powdered ay betwene."

In Tudor and Stuart times the peony was a universal favourite and Gerard, who gives eight illustrations of the varieties, mentions that all of them were commonly grown in London gardens. Parkinson in his *Paradisus* says of them "They are endenizened in our gardens where we cherish them for the beauty and delight of their goodly flowers as well as for their physical vertues." Five varieties of the iris, another flower of ancient lineage, are depicted in the "Summer garden." The earliest known illustration of an iris is probably that in the famous Vienna Codex of Dioscorides compiled in the early part of the sixth century.

To lovers of carnations and pinks perhaps the most attractive of these engravings are those of the flowers Perdita described as "the fairest flowers o' the season". Carnations and pinks derive their generic name from *caryophyllus* owing to their clove-like scent. Chaucer speaks of "many a clove gelofre and note muge to put in ale" but it is more probably to the spice he refers. "Gelofre" which later became "gilly flower" is possibly a French corruption of caryophyllon but according to William Lawson [*The New Orchard and Garden* 1618] gilly flower is "July flower". "July flowres, commonly called Gilly-flowers or Clove July-flowres [I call them so because they flowre in July] they have the name of Cloves of their scent and the best sort of them are called Queen-July-flowres. I have of them nine or ten severall colours and divers of them as bigge as Roses: of all flowres [save the Damaske Rose] they are the most pleasant to sight and smell." Gillyflowers are mentioned by Tusser, by Hyll in his *Proffitable Arte of Gardening* and in Lyte's Herbal. When carnations and pinks were first cultivated in English gardens is uncertain. *Dianthus caryophyllus* grows wild in the south of Europe and as a naturalised wild plant in parts of England. The Ancient Romans are supposed to have spiced wine with the clove scented dianthus and according to tradition this variety was brought to Italy by soldiers in Caesar Augustus' army from the northern shores of Spain before the Christian era. By the middle of the sixteenth century the flower had evidently been greatly improved for Turner in his Herbal says of them "They are made pleasant and swete with the labours and will of man and not by nature."

The variety commonly known as "Sweet William" were called *Cayophyllus Carthusianorum* or *lychnis monachorum hortensis* in the sixteenth century and these names suggest that they were introduced into England in the twelfth century by the Carthusian monks. According to tradition they took their name from William the Conqueror. The varieties of sweet Williams with narrow leaves were formerly called "sweet Johns." The meaning of the word 'carnation' is doubtful. Both in Spenser's *Shepherds Calendar* and in lyte's Herbal it is spelt 'coronation' and according to some the flower gets its name from the fact that garlands were commonly made of it. Clusius mentions yellow and apricot coloured carnations being sold in the market place of Vienna and Gerard describes a yellow carnation which he says was sent from Poland.

In the sixteenth and seventeenth centuries the carnation vied with the rose in popularity. Gerard in his *Herball* [1597] expresses astonishment that so beautiful a flower was not mentioned by the ancient Greek and Roman authors. "It is marvell" he says "that such a famous flower, so pleasant and sweete, should lie hid, and not be made knowen by the olde writers, which may be thought not inferior to the Rose in beautie; smell and varietie." Parkinson in his *Paradisus* writes with equal enthusiasm of "the

Queene of delight and of flowers, Carnations and Gilliflowers, whose bravery, variety and sweete smell joyned together, tyeth every ones affection with great earnestnesse both to like and to have them" and many of those he depicts have delightful names – 'Master Tuggie's Princesse', 'Lustie Gallant', 'Master Bradshawe his daintie Ladie', 'Fair Maid of Kent'.

Carnations and gilly flowers were used extensively both for flavouring and in medicine. The variety known as 'sops in wine' were so called because wine was flavoured with them when they were in flower. In *The Queen's Closet Opened* the author, who was cook to Queen Henrietta Maria, gives a recipe for making gillyflower wine. Syrups and conserves were made of the flowers and the petals were candied like rose petals. Many of the old gardening writers give curiously unpractical directions for altering and improving the scent of carnations. Gervase Markham says "Now if you will have your Gilliflowers of divers smels or odours, you may also with great ease, as thus for example: if you will take two or three great cloves and steepe them foure and twenty houres in Damaske Rose-water, then take them out and bruise them, and put them into a fine Cambricke ragge and so binde them about the roote of the Gillyflower neere to the setting on of the stalke, and so plant it in a fine, soft and fertile mould, and the flower which springeth from the same will have so delicate a mixt smell of the Clove and the Rose-water that it will breed both delight and wonder." The use of these flowers in medicine was manifold. William Coles in *Adam in Eden* writes 'The conserve made of the flowers and sugar is exceeding cordiall, and wonderfully above measure doth comfort the heart, being eaten now and then, which is very good also against the plague or any kind of venome. It is likewise good not only for the falling sicknesse, palsy, giddiness, and the cramp, but for the pestilence.... The syrup of the said flowers strengthens the heart, refresheth the vital spirits and is a good cordial in feavers, expelling the poyson and fury of the disease, and greatly comforting those that are sick of any other disease, where the heart hath need of relief. Moreover, the leaves of the flowers, put into a glasse of vinegar, and set in the sun for certain dayes, do make a pleasant vinegar, and very good to revive one of a swoon, the nostrills and temples being washed therewith."

Parkinson was the first to attempt a classification of carnations and gillyflowers. The large flowered varieties he called carnations, the smaller gillyflowers and the yellow 'orange tawnies'. It is interesting to recall that carnations were the first plants on which hybridisation was practised. Richard Bradley in his *New Improvements of Planting and Gardening* [1717] writes "The Carnation and Sweet William are in some respects alike: the farina of one will impregnate the other, and the seed so enlivened will produce a plant differing from either, as may be now seen in the garden of Mr. Thomas Fairchild, resembling both equally, which was raised from the seed of a Carnation that had been impregnated by the farina of the Sweet William."

One of the most attractive engravings is that of the hollyhock. In Tudor and Stuart times both the single and double varieties were cultivated. One of the most charming descriptions of this flower is to be found in Hyll's *Proffitable Arte of Gardening.* "The greater or Garden Mallowes is like in beautie unto the rose, although not so strong of savour, and sweete of smell, which the women in our time use to decke their houses and windowes with. And the floure doth both open at the full appearance of the Sunne and shutteth again at the setting of the Sunne." Parkinson observes that "they sute you with flowers when almost you have no other to grace out your Garden". John Lawrence in his *Flower Garden* [1726] says that owing to their great height "proper Places against Walls or the Corners of Gardens should be assigned to them where they may explain their Beauty to distant Views". Hollyhocks in the sixteenth and seventeenth centuries were frequently called mallows. They are of the Mallow tribe and in olden times the leaves of both were used as pot-herbs. Evelyn however says "they are only commended by some". From the earliest times the whole mallow family have been renowned for their healing properties and it is a tradition that when the ordeal of holding a red-hot iron was inflicted the suspected person covered his hands with a paste made of marsh mallows and white of egg and was thereby enabled to hold a red-hot iron for a moment with impunity.

The engravings of lilies and roses are singularly beautiful. The Madonna lily is one of the oldest flowers cultivated in England and its medicinal virtues were well known to our Saxon ancestors. Bartholomaeus Anglicus, one of the greatest scholars of the Middle Ages, gives a beautiful description of the flower. A fifteenth century translation of the latin original reads thus—"The lily is an hearbe with a white flower: And though the leaves of the floure be white, yet within shineth the likenesse of golde. The Lily is next to the Rose in worthiness and noblenes....Nothing is more gracious than the lily in fairnes of colour, in sweetnesse of smell, and in effect of working and vertue." Walafred Strabo in the ninth century wrote of lilies "Who can describe the exceeding whiteness of the lily? The rose it should be crowned with pearls of Arabia and Lydian gold. Better and sweeter are these flowers than all other plants and rightly called the flower of flowers. Yes roses and lilies, the one for virginity with no sordid toil, no warmth of love, but the glow of their own sweet scent, which spreads further than the rival roses, but once bruised or crushed turns all to rankness. Therefore roses and lilies for our church, one for the martyrs' blood, the other for the symbol in his hand. Pluck them O maiden, roses for war and lilies for peace, and think of that Flower of the stem of Jesse. Lilies His words were, and the hallowed acts of His pleasant life, but His death re-dyed the roses".

The roses depicted are the roses prized by our ancestors for their delicious scent and now alas rarely seen. The Damask rose is the wild rose of Damascus and there is little doubt that it was introduced into Europe by the Crusaders. Rosamundi, the variety of the damask rose striped with white takes it name from Henry II's mistress Fair Rosamund. Nicholas Monardus describes this rose as 'inter album et rubrum'. The hundred leaved rose described by Theophrastus and Pliny is the 'provincial' rose of Shakespeare and the same as the deliciously scented cabbage rose formerly grown in every cottage garden. This rose was probably the original of the red rose of the House of Lancaster. Edmund Langley, second son of Henry III of England, held the fief of Champagne from the French King and was sent to avenge the murder of the Mayor of Provins. The prince on his return to England adopted the red rose of Provins for his device, this being the hundred leaved rose introduced by Thibault Comte de Brie from Syria. The rose which Shakespeare describes as "the rose damasked red and white" is the York and Lancaster rose. The true variety of this deliciously scented rose is quite six feet high when full grown and blooms lavishly.

Musk roses and sweet briar were also highly valued for their scent. The sweet briar is the 'eglantine' of Spenser, Shakespeare, Bacon and Milton, and of it Bacon says it yields "the sweetest smell in the air". According to Hakluyt the musk rose was introduced into this country in the sixteenth century. Shakespeare associates both musk roses and sweet briar with the fairy queen.

"With sweet musk roses and with eglantine:
There sleeps Titania, sometime of the night,
Lull'd in these flowers with dances and delight."

ELEANOUR SINCLAIR ROHDE.

NOTE ON THE TRANSLATIONS.

In order to make these translations more readable, it has been necessary to resort to a certain amount of interpretation. The use of the words petal, stamen, anther, pistil and stigma belongs to a later period than that of the *Hortus Floridus*; but these terms have been employed here only when there was no doubt that the author had observed and noted the particular part of the plant in question. In some instances the same Latin terms that would be used today occur in the texts; but it should not be forgotten that an English Translator in 1614 would have rendered them somewhat differently. The adoption of Latin botanical terms as English words belongs to a comparatively late period. Although it would be desirable in a highly critical translation of these texts to endeavour to give the meaning in English words similar to those which would have been used by a contemporary of Crispin Van de Pass, in the present instance the aim has been to indicate the extent to which a first-hand observation of plants has been recorded.

S. SAVAGE.

SUMMER

of the

HORTUS FLORIDUS

in which the principal flowers of Summer are portrayed to the very

life by the excellent graver of

CRISPIN VAN DE PASS.

The Great Female Pæone.

I t was called *Pæonia* from Pæon its discoverer; and *Glycisida* from the Grecian authors because it was seen to have seeds similar to those of a pomegranate. The stems of the female pæony, unlike those of the male, are but little or not at all reddened; the leaves, down-drooping as in *hipposelinion* [which Theophrastus called *Smyrnion*], for the most part not only divided, but also strikingly narrower than in the male pæony, greener on the upper surfaces, and waxing paler underneath. The flowers are very large, brightly flaming with crimson, luxuriant in the number of their petals, as many as two hundred being enclosed within the orbit of each flower. The dark, rounded seeds are in husks similar to those of the almond; some of which seeds are resplendent with a scarlet colour, but less so than in the male pæony. Many glandulous roots descend from one centre, similar to the roots of the true asphodel, but much thicker and longer; from which often are sent forth two or three rootlets, always of the same shape. It flowers in the month of May, an ornament of gardens.

1. Paeonia fœm: maxim:.

II
'The Greater Iris of Dodoens.

The Iris, so called from its likeness to the rainbow, which its flowers resemble not only in colour but in dignity, produces diverse kinds. The leaves of this Greater Iris are rather long, like unto swords. Its stems are rounded, smooth, a cubit high [some higher], at the tops of which are placed flowers in alternate order, three or four in number, and scented. These flowers consist mainly of six petals, of which three are reflexed downwards, bent in the manner of a bow, pale coloured on the under surfaces, but on the upper surfaces resembling very nearly the most lovely colour of the black violet, intermingled with white lines arising from each golden fringe; the other three petals, fainter in colour, are curved upwards one against another. Each fringe, like a separate flower, arises in its own part of the petal, and adheres to the cup of the flower, and from thence is extended up and down from its own middle, as though by many, narrow, short, yellowish hairs, in shape like those of the hairy *Eruca*. Besides these, and in front of the six petals, are three other oblong, narrow petals, cleft in two at top, which each fringe somewhat hides. Under each of these petals is a single stamen. The roots of this Iris are oblong, solid, jointed, of the thickness of a finger, often distributed in many layers.

L. *Iris maior.*
I. *Giglio.*
G. *Glacyul.*
Ge. *Lifch.*

III
The SUSIAN IRIS.

This Iris, one of the broad leaved Irises, was first brought to us from Constantinople. It is called by the Turks *Alaga Susam* because it was believed to grow abundantly around the city of Susa in Persia. It has six or eight leaves similar to those of the two-flowered Spanish Iris, a rounded stem quite a foot and a half high, or higher, with a swelling from which arises the flower, larger than in other Irises, composed of nine petals; of which three, thick and reflexed, are somewhat blackish to purple, adorned with small somewhat whitish veins and covered with black hairs, resembling a silken garment sprinkled over with dark spots of a like colour. Leaning on these are three petals tending less towards black and as it were from black merging to purple. The three broad uprising petals, somewhat thin, are partly of an ashen colour, spotted, with countless little lines and furrows running together, as is seen in the extended tail of the Guinea hen. This flower is valued on account of its colour, but usually it has no scent; and is a plant which blooms more rarely because less able to endure the cold. Often with us, after its first flower, it is hardly ever seen to bloom again in the same season.

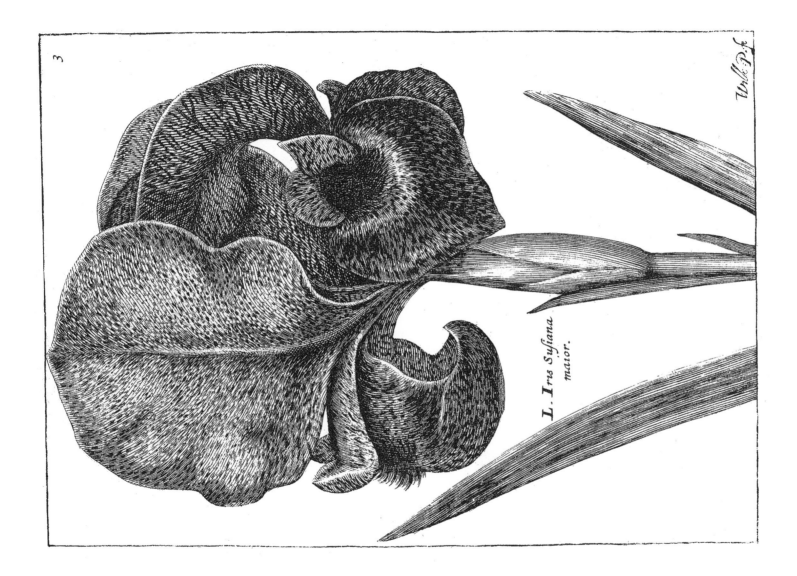

I. *Iris Sufiana maior.*

THE NARROW LEAVED IRIS OF CLUSIUS.

This narrow leaved Iris not unhappily may be called the Pannonian Parti-coloured Iris, as it is abundant in Hungary and Upper Austria. In elegance it does not yield place to any other Iris. It has leaves more than a foot and a half high, narrow in shape, not exceeding the width of the little finger; merging to greenness at the tips and towards the ground somewhat tending to purple; not of a pleasant smell. The stems sometimes rise to three feet high, and are rounded, strong, hollow, and jointed; divided in the upper part into two or three branches, from which the pleasant scented flowers come forth, differing but little from the parti-coloured flowers of the broad leaved bulbous Irises; the three downward-bent petals showing a dusky colour underneath, and on the upper surfaces a violet colour abounding with intermingling lines and veins of a delightful purple, a golden line taking the place of a fringe; and the three erect petals, less broad and not very much curved towards one another, are decorated with a full sky-blue or a purple colour. The roots are crooked, knotted, and intertwined, sending down many slender rootlets.

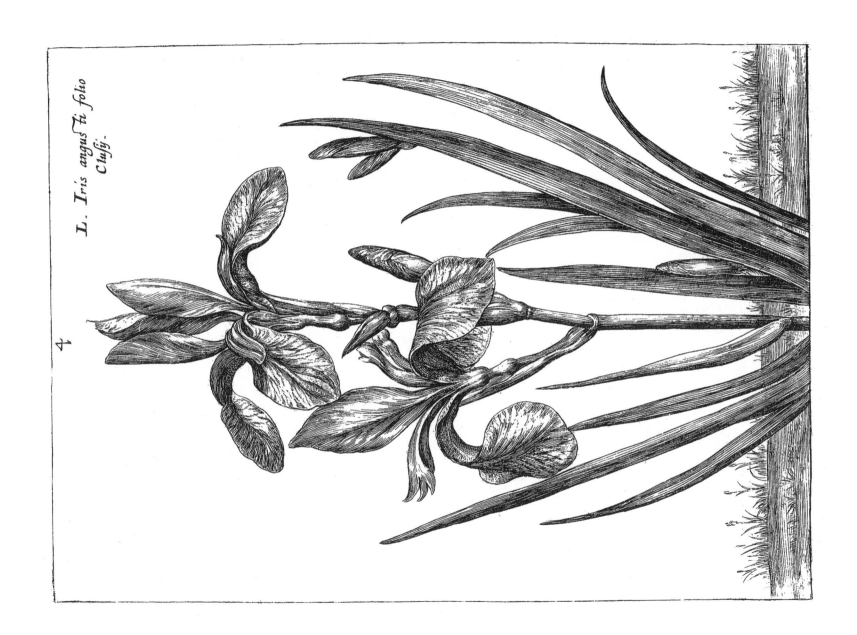

L. Iris angustifolio
Clusii.

4

THE GREATER SISYNRICHIUM. THE BROAD-LEAVED BULBOUS IRIS.

V

The Greater *Sisynrichium* is provided with rather long and narrow leaves, more supple than the leaves of the bulbous Iris and coming nearest to those of *Hyacinthus botryodes*, grooved, green in colour, and often lying along the ground; also with a rounded stem, grooved and strong, nine inches high, which from many wrappings — as it were from little sheaths — sends forth flowers four or five in number, produced alternately: when the first withers, the next succeeds it, then a third, and so on: resembling rather the flower of *Xyris* than of *Iris*, and composed of nine petals. Three of the petals are bent downwards, and in place of a fringe have a yellow spot; three others are raised somewhat upwards; but the remaining three, which arising among the other three are wont to hide their tips, are divided in the upper part and cleft in two. But the whole flower is beautiful to behold, of a sky-blue colour except for the yellow spots; and is in truth of excellent though rather fleeting scent. The round and somewhat reddish seed is contained in a thin skin. The bulbous root is as it were double.

The Broad-leaved Bulbous Iris, described by Clusius and also by Dodoens, has broad leaves similar to those of the non-bulbous lilies, supple and of a quince colour; among which rises a short stem on which appears a flower of the shape of other bulbous Irises, of pleasant scent, and of a somewhat pale sky-blue colour. When the first flower has died away, two others come forth, one on either side. In shape the root is like that of the onion, sweet of taste, and composed of manifold rinds somewhat blackish in colour.

.S.

L. Iris Bulbosa latif: Clusij.

L. Syfinrichium
maius.

THE YELLOW FLOWERED BULBOUS IRIS. THE SPANISH BULBOUS IRIS.

VI

This first Bulbous Iris has rather long, narrow, grooved leaves, four or five in number tolerably like those of the yellow asphodel, hollow in the upper part but in the lower part extended and somewhat rounded; a stem a cubit high; a flower at the top, of an elegant yellow colour, composed of six larger and three smaller petals, to which as it were a thick oblong pod follows after, in which is the seed. The oblong bulbous root is covered by a somewhat reddish skin, and as soon as the flower is produced becomes two bulbs, with the [new] stem arising from the lower part and from the rootlets of the bulb.

The Spanish kind differs not particularly in shape from the preceding; but the reflexed petals are white below, and the uprising ones bear a sky-blue colour. Narrower and smaller than the lower petals, the upper ones so lean upon them that neither the stamens nor the anthers can be seen; also they appear to cling together, their tops being cleft and turned back.

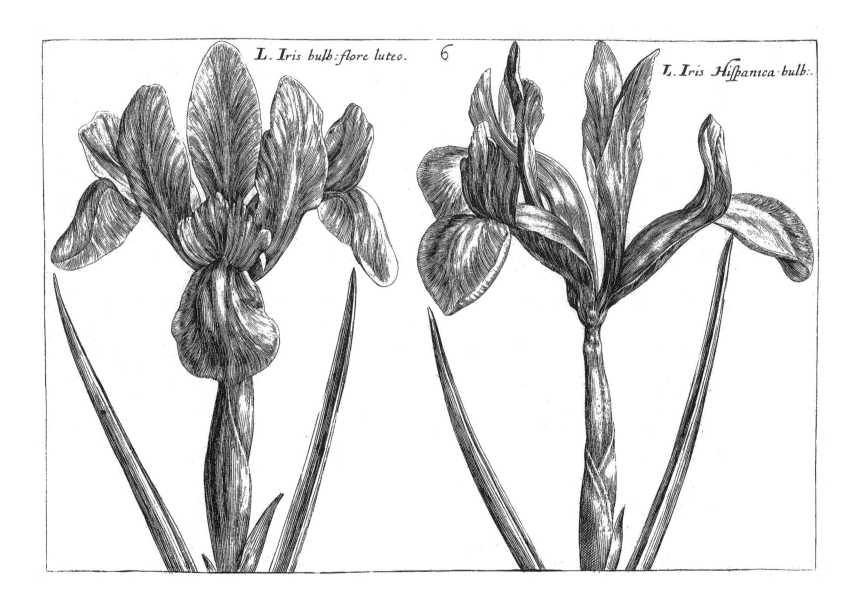

L. Iris bulb: flore luteo.   6   L. Iris Hispanica bulb:

VII
MOUNTAIN MOLY.

BROAD-LEAVED, WITH A YELLOW FLOWER.   NARROW LEAVED.

The Broad-leaved Moly is so called from its broad, thick, gross, keel bearing, and erect leaves, which do not differ much from those of *Scylla*, and are like in colour to the leek. Its stem is a foot high, and green; producing at the top, from a thin membrane consisting of two leaflets, more than thirty petals, six together standing out firmly on each of the slender stems; which separate star-shaped flowerets are composed of six petals outwardly pale but inwardly yellow, in the middle of which projects a style divided into three parts, surrounded regularly by six yellow stamens, with anthers of the same colour. The root is bulbous, like that of the leek, and is often double.

The other Moly here portrayed, called Narrow-leaved from its narrower and somewhat rush-like leaves, puts forth down-hanging flowerets similar to those of the first, but a clear white in colour, and gracefully decorated with little purple veins.

7

L. Moly latifolium mont: flore flavo.

L. Moly mōtan: angustifolium.

VIII
THE MOUNTAIN LILY.

This wild lily called *Lilium montanum* puts forth rounded stems two cubits high or higher, long broad and pointed leaves not disposed one above another in uncertain order but at certain places on the stem, encompassing it in the form of a radiant star. The flowers hang downwards from their own stems, with the cleft of a lily, but smaller than in others, faded purple in colour and brilliant with purple speckles, the stamens in the centre being of the same colour. The petals are reflexed and turned backwards almost in a circle. The bulbous roots, like many kernels joined together, are of a golden or yellow colour, [on account of which the French have called the whole plant by the name of Lis jaune], from which rootlets hang down. According to Fuchs and Gesner, it grows in woods and on mountains in many places in Germany. The Dutch have it with other lilies in their gardens. It flowers at about the beginning of June, preceding the white lilies.

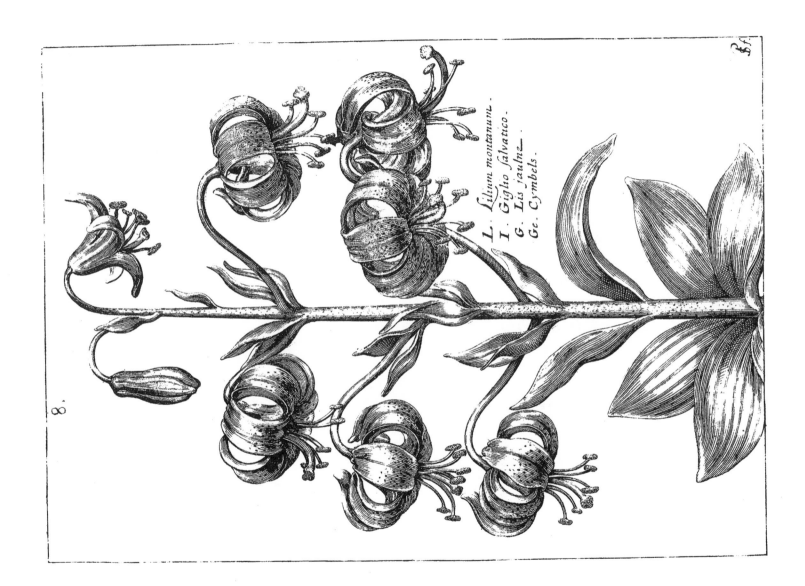

8

L. *Lilium montanum.*
I. *Giglio salvatico.*
G. *Lis jaune.*
Ge. *Cymbels.*

THE LILY CALLED IX MARTAGON POMPONII.

This lily, called *Martagon Pomponii* for a long time by those who have grown it, by which name they, themselves claimed to have received it from Italy, is still rare in these provinces, because in growing it increases itself with the greatest difficulty. Nor has seed been known to have been displayed by the plant, save that Clusius, in his Appendix, writes that about the year 1606 he himself obtained ten or twelve compact, flat, circular, small, reddish seeds, from pods combined in a six-fold series. However, this lily from the woodlands has a prominent stem more than a foot and a half high, surrounded by very many rather long and narrow leaves in confused order. In the upper part of the stem the flowers grow alternately from their own stems, and are somewhat of a rich saffron or red-lead colour, with their petals reflexed and turned backwards almost in a circle. The root is bulbous. Indeed, this plant is rather abundant in the blooming of its flowers, for it is reported to have had nearly or more than thirty-six in number.

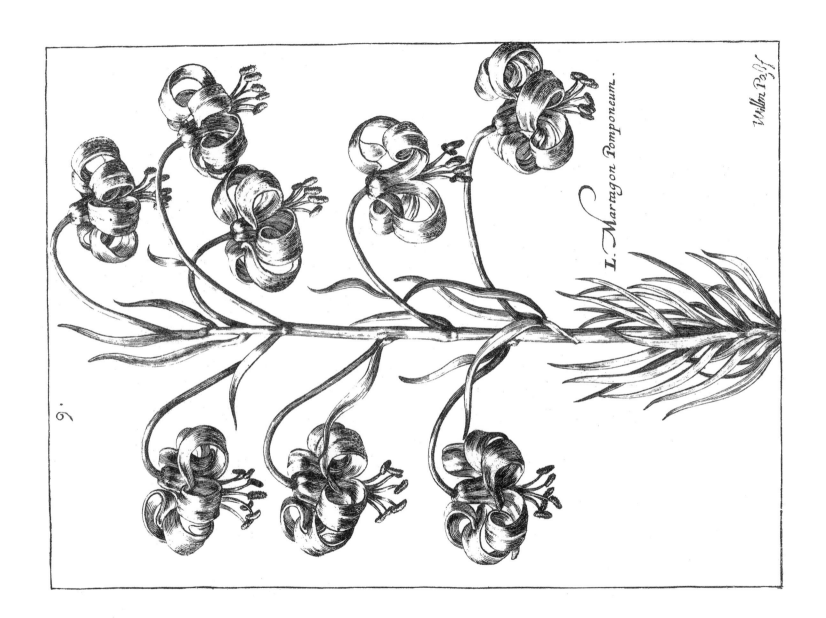

I. Martagon Pomponeum.

Willm Paff

X
THE BULB-BEARING RED LILY.

This red or purple Lily is seen to be one of the larger lilies. It has a tall stem, and leaves similar to those of *Lilium album*, but with many darker and narrower ones round about the stem, though none before its rising up; also many flowers at the top of the stem, arranged one above another in uncertain order, in shape like those of the white lily, but inclining from red to saffron in colour, besprinkled as it were with many little black punctures like the beginnings of certain letters. The roots are large bulbs composed of many kernels, as those of the white lily but larger.

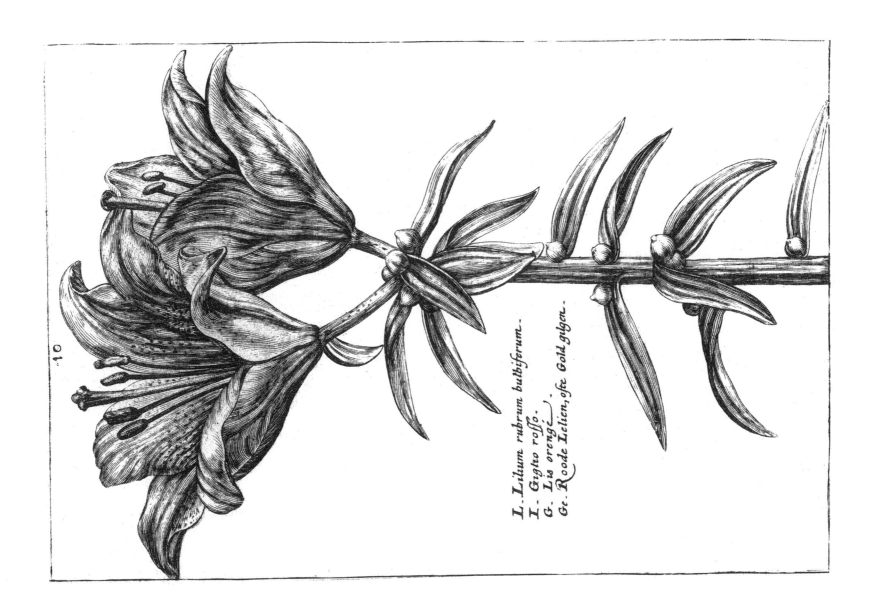

L. *Lilium rubrum bulbiferum.*
I. *Giglio rosso.*
G. *Lis orengé.*
Ge. *Roode Lelien, ofte Gold gilgen.*

THE GLADIOLUS XI OR SWORD FLAG

OF NARBONNE. WITH FLOWERS ON BOTH SIDES.

The leaves of *Gladiolus* are rather long, narrow, grooved, pointed in a sword-like fashion, smaller and narrower than those of *Iris*. The stem is smooth, rounded, more than a cubit high, close to which are at the most six or seven flowers, separate in order one above another, and arranged at one side of the stem. Each flower has six petals joined together, a ruddy purple in colour or [which is nevertheless rare] of a clear white. Afterwards there follow the oblong rounded pods, the seeds in which are thin and chaff-like. The root is a double bulb, one fixed above the other; of which the upper one is smaller and more vigorous at the beginning of spring, the lower one being larger but more flaccid. A little later on, the lower bulb disappears, thereupon being increased into many bulbs.

After this first sort [which has been described above] there follows the other kind called by de Lobel *Gladiolus italicus*, with two rows of flowers, or well enough in other words, with flowers on both sides of the stem meeting together with one higher than the rest.

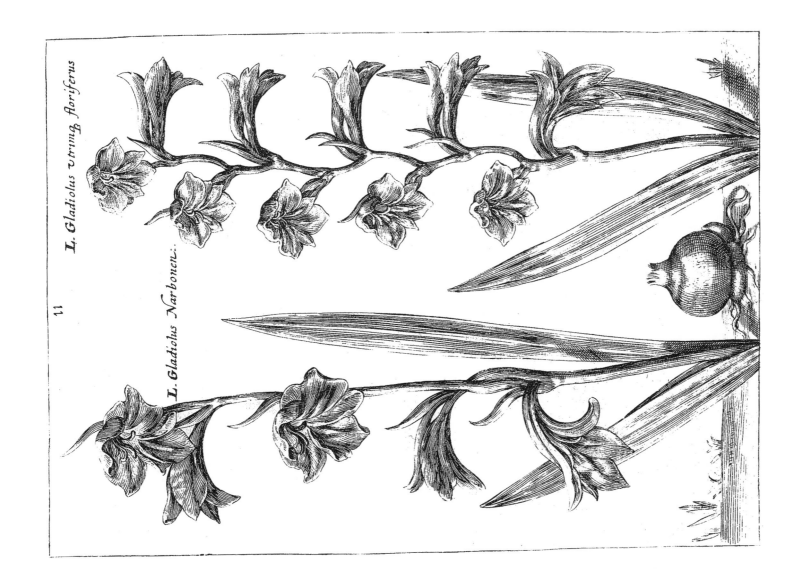

11

L. Gladiolus utrin_g, floriferus

L. Gladiolus Narbonen.

THE WHITE ROSE WITH A FULL FLOWER. THE RED PRÆNESTIAN ROSE.

XII

Among all flowers the Rose easily holds the first place; and its use in all manner of garlands is almost beyond measure. Moreover, it is the most sung of in poets' verses, and blossoming seems to spread its immortal fragrance throughout so many graceful writings today.

The greater part of this variety of plants is abundant. In a census of planted roses this first one exceeds the rest in the tallness of its stems or branches; bearing clear white flowers with many petals, extremely sweet-smelling. But the Prænestian Rose, which follows it, is shorter, with branches two cubits high or higher; and has a flower in truth finely red,—but less so than that of the Milesian Rose,— with a remarkable manifold arrangement of the petals, and a grateful and extremely delightful scent.

Rosa alba ple:flo: 12.   *L. Rosa rubra praeneſtina.*

THE DUTCH ROSE OF A HUNDRED XIII PETALS.. THE PARTI-COLOURED ROSE.

Rosa centifolia, so called from the number of petals in its flower, and *Batavica* from the region in which it grows abundantly, was not unknown to the ancients, seeing that the most celebrated writers have borne it in mind. Theophrastus wrote of it in his History of Plants; Pliny in his Natural History; and Athenœus, in his work "Dipnosophistarum", to what an extent it was found in the Campania of Italy and about Philippi in Greece. Clusius in several places mentions that he himself counted the petals of the flower, the larger outer ones, and the inner very little ones filling the place in the middle with filaments; and also that the leaves of the cup itself are reflexed. Moreover, he perceived that the scent was like that of the white rose; also that the colour was not very unlike that of the Prœnestian Rose, although fainter.

This other fine rose is seen to be of the same stock as the Prœnestian Rose, similar in form and size; and most commonly has petals with one half partly of a clear white, the rest red; or they are observed to be only with one third partly of a dull white, then of a pure white, then of a pure red, intermingled.

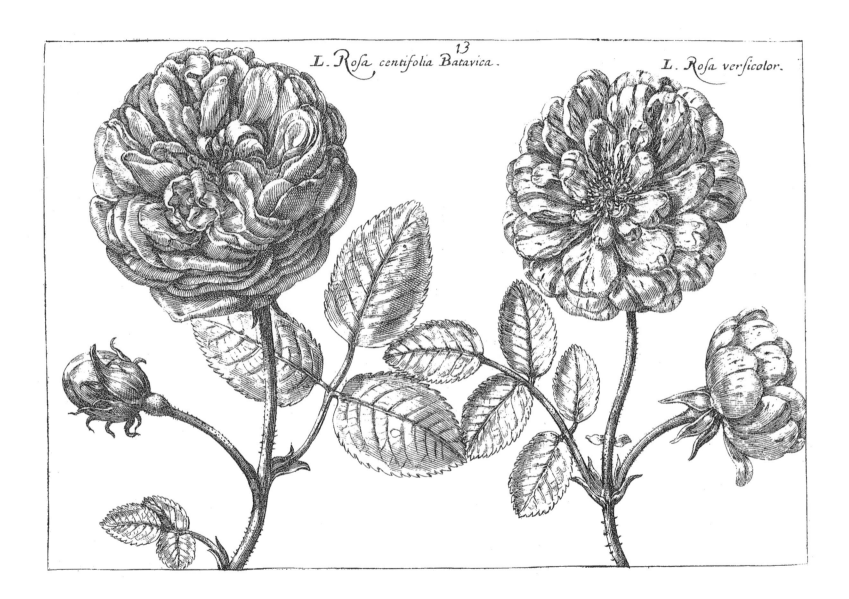

L. Rosa centifolia Batavica.
13
L. Rosa versicolor.

XIV
CAMPANULAS, OR CANTERBURY BELLS.

These plants, usually called Campanulas, of which three sorts are noted by Dodoens, are seen to have a certain likeness to the wild rampions. The greater or giant one, portrayed here first, has broad first leaves, in shape like those of the black violet, although larger; but it puts forth close to the stems which are strong enough, and on both sides of them, more oblong leaves of a deep green. After the stems, very many flowers are produced, larger and more open than the flowers of *Rapunculus*, almost like little bells, beautiful with a sky-blue colour, and with clear white stamens in their centres. The root in the young plants is of the thickness of a finger and oblong, but in the old plants divided into many rootlets.

The latter sort here portrayed is smaller, having everywhere narrow and oblong leaves bright with a deep green colour. The grooved stems are two cubits high; and around the upper parts grow flowers like enough to the first sort, but a clear white in colour.

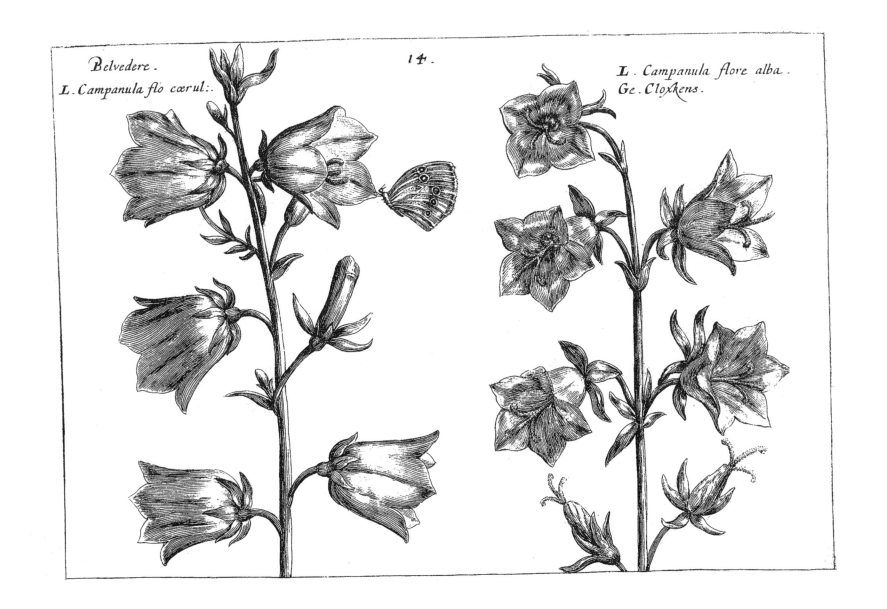

Belvedere.
L. Campanula flo cœrul:.

14.

L. Campanula flore alba.
Ge. Cloxkens.

THE POPPY WITH A MANIFOLD FLOWER.

XV

These two sorts of Poppies endowed with a full flower strike the eyes of the beholders. Both agree in their oblong leaves, saw-like along the edges and joined to the stem without stalks. Which stem is in truth straight and smooth, four or five feet high, producing a splendid flower, with broad petals at its outer edge and filled in the middle with countless smaller petals crowded together, of a clear white or a somewhat whitish colour. It abounds in seed, which at maturity freely escapes from the chinks in the little knob-like head.

The other poppy puts forth a flower not less in size or gracefulness, full of countless little petals split at their ends, and tinted with a dark purple or somewhat flesh colour; to which, similarly as with the first poppy, seeds grow abundantly in the little heads.

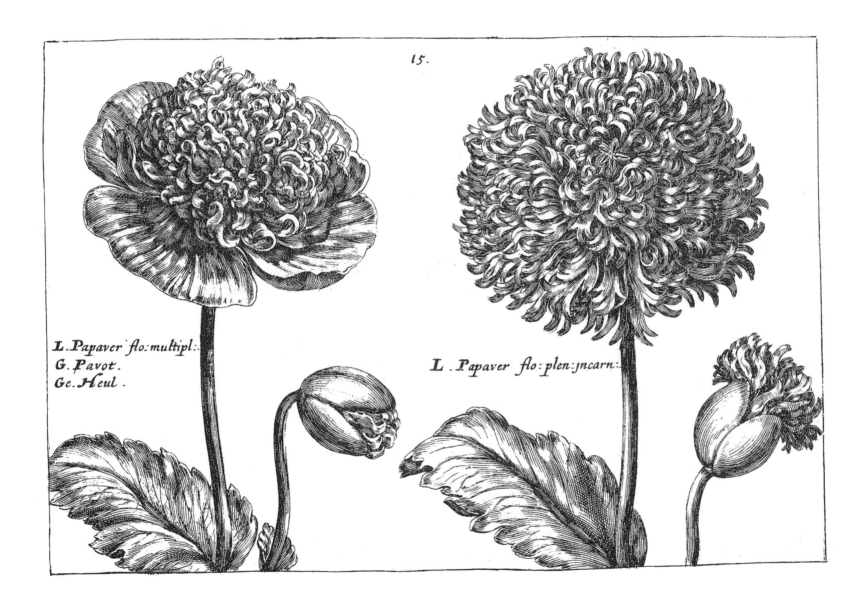

15.

L. Papaver flo: multipl:.
G. Pavot.
Ge. Heul.

L. Papaver flo: plen: jncarn:

XVI
THE GARLAND CAMPION,

WITH A WHITE FLOWER.   WITH A FULL RED FLOWER.

The Garland *Lychnis* bears oblong leaves, a thumb's width or a little broader, soft, woolly and grey, smaller indeed than the leaves of *Verbascum* but whiter and more woolly. The stems are a cubit high, rounded, jointed, grey, and likewise woolly, divided into many short wings. On the tops of the stems are separate flowers, each in its own cup, but unscented, larger than the flowers of the dame's violet; and although usually with five petals, and very rarely with six, not crowded with many except in the flower with manifold petals. The anthers in the centre of the flowers are sharp and pricking. The roots are slender underneath. It is planted in gardens in the Low Countries, and flowers almost throughout the summer.

This *Lychnis* put in the first place* has a simple flower, a clear white in colour; but the other shows the full-flowered one, which has many gleaming petals of a red colour and like unto a flame of fire.

* [This description was probably made from the drawing, and not from the engraving, as the flowers are in reverse order.]

134   SUMMER

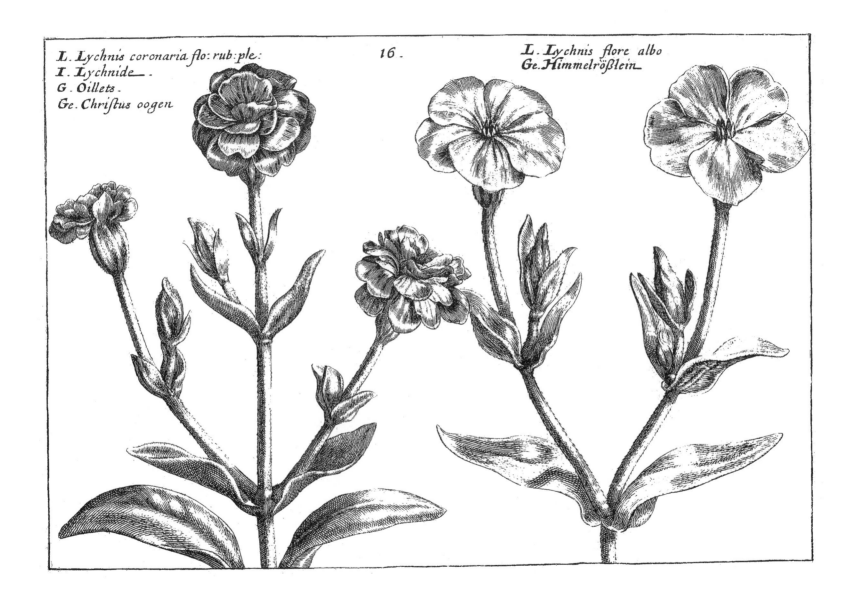

L. *Lychnis coronaria flo: rub:ple:*
I. *Lychnide*.
G. *Oillets*.
Ge. *Christus oogen*

16.

L. *Lychnis flore albo*
Ge. *Himmelrößlein*

THE SMALLER GILLIFLOWER, OR PINK,

This is another and smaller kind of *Caryophylleus*, with slender stems and leaves very similar to those of the larger kinds, but smaller in both respects; also having similar flowers from little oblong rounded cups, but likewise smaller, in their outer edges more slit, and fringed in the likeness of little downy feathers [from which with the Dutch the plant derives its name]. The flowers are of a clear white in colour, or from whiteness tending to purple or to flesh colour. Some name this plant *Veronica altilis* or *Coronaria minor aut altera*, on account of the lovely elegance of its flowers, which are sought after by all.

L. Superba alba.

L. Superba flo: simp:.

XVIII
GREAT GILLIFLOWERS, OR CARNATIONS,
WHITE VARIEGATED WITH PURPLE SPOTS.   COMPLETELY BLOOD RED.
A PURE SNOW-WHITE.

The stems of the larger *Caryophylleus flos* are smooth, rounded and jointed, a cubit high, or higher. The leaves are in pairs from each of the joints. They are oblong, hard, narrow, pointed at the ends, and almost of a bluish grey in colour. The lovely flowers, in their long, rounded, and pronged cups, are usually of six petals in the single kinds, but in the double kinds of very many petals joined together, pliantly fringed and very much cut into. It is evident that those here portrayed show very great differences in the variety of their colours. The flowers have a very sweet scent, recalling the fragrant Indian cloves; and from the centre of the petals there project two clear white stigmas. The small, black seed is in little oblong vessels. The stringy roots endure for many years, and may be almost safe against the rigours of winter.

18

L.Caryophilus flore albo punctato.

L.Cariophilus flore sanguineo.

L.Caryophylus flore niveo.

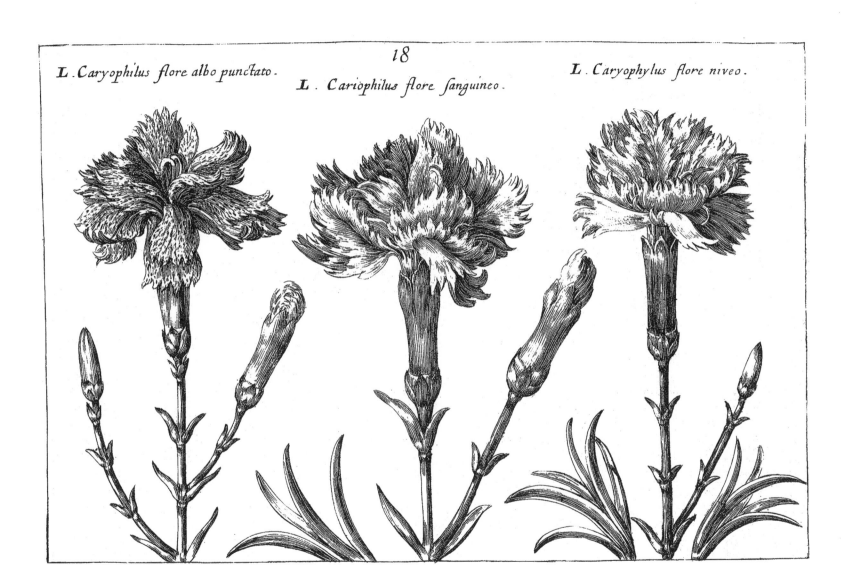

XIX
NIGELLA, OR GITH.

Three kinds of *Melanthium* are for the most part taken account of. Here we show the common one, and the one with a full flower described by Clusius. The stem in the sown or garden kinds of nigella is short, and provided with slender grass-like branchlets, more than nine inches in height, having small leaves divided into slender, oblong parts, like those of the herb "senecio" but much more meagre. In the tops of the branchlets arise little flowers with clear white petals, having many stamens at the centre, and five or six separate recepticles intermingled at the inner side but horn-shaped outwardly, in which [in due season] are enclosed the angular, black, sharp-tasting, scented seeds.

Melanthium odorum pleno flore, so named by Clusius, differs little from the first here portrayed; nevertheless, the flowers, from a dull white to a somewhat greenish colour, are more abundant in the number of their petals, which are nine or ten in number and sometimes overlapping one another; also with their edges somewhat cleft.

19

L. Melanthium flore simplici.

L. Melanthium flore pleno

XX
GIANT GILLIFLOWERS, OR CARNATIONS.
Flesh coloured, and marked with slight spots.   Striped with scarlet and snow white.

Ruellius believed that *Caryophylleus flos*, of which we have previously given some pictures, was not unknown to the ancients. But in our own times it is so very frequent, aye, and considering the infinite variety of its kinds, it gives place to no other flower, nor yields the honour, be it for elegance of colour and form, or for the fragrance of its sweet scent. Here we add two more plants, at once excellent in size and gracefulness, of which the leaves are broad and ample, and the stems so in proportion. The flower of the first one has petals of flesh colour, with the edges deeply cleft, and marked with almost invisible scarlet spots. The petals of the other one are nearly of the same size, of scarlet and dull white colours intermingled and adorned by lines playing together in a certain manner, like unto little flames of fire; and they also have their edges beautifully notched. It is not without cause that it is believed that weariness of the eyes is refreshed in the joy of beholding this flower. The most excellent young man Fr. Buchomius, who is wont to be allured not a little by these sports of nature, has communicated these two flowers to me.

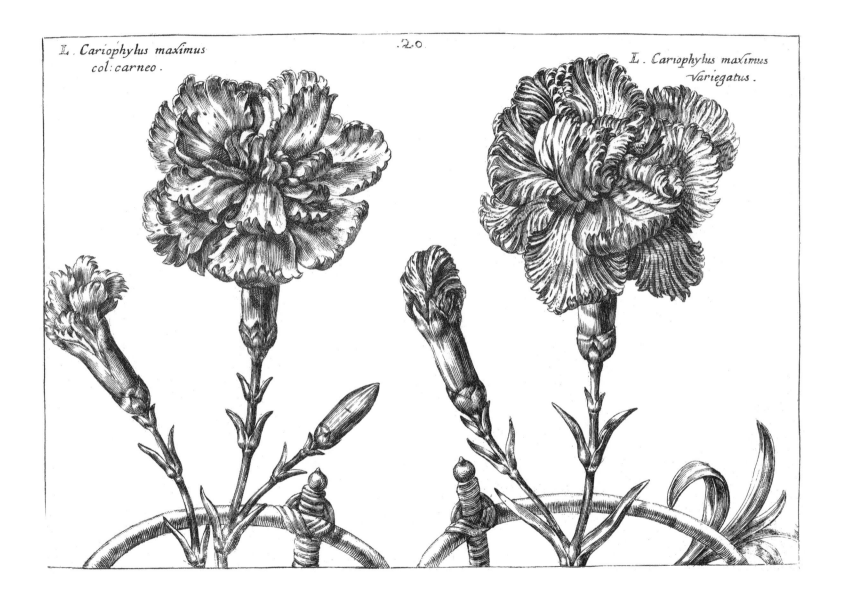

20

L. *Cariophylus maximus*
col: carneo.

L. *Cariophylus maximus*
Variegatus.

AUTUMN

of the

hORTUS FLORIDUS

containing the rarer autumn flowers engraved by the excellent

diligence and exertion of

CRISPIN VAN DE PASS ThE YOUNGER.

Epigramma.

FLORA naturæ reserans receſs,
Exhibet blandas violas, roſasq̃,
Quicquid et dites Arabes remittũt.
    Spargit odorum.

B.

Simon Paſſæus sculp: vlt

DODOENS' OTHER SORT OF CLEMATIS WITH A PURPLE FLOWER.

Clematis altera described by Dodoens, also called in Greek Έπιγηῖτις, and in Latin *Ambuxum*, usually blossoms in the autumn. It grows aloft, with long, slender, knotty, reddish branches, which, assuredly like those of the ivy, cling to trees and other neighbouring objects. Its many leaves are cleft and separate, broad, veined, and not unlike those of the first *Flammula* [*=Clematis*]; sharp and hot in taste. The flowers are large and very graceful, hanging forward separately from the ends of slender branchlets; and composed of only four petals in the form of a decussate cross, purple in colour—sometimes rather approaching a dark blue, sometimes towards a red. Some hairy stamens occupy the centre of the flower. The seed is flat, and borne in little rounded heads, and is provided with a long, hairy, bent tail; which seed matures in the autumn. The root is oblong and slender, spreading out sidelong yellowish fibres. In Italy and Spain it grows freely by the sides of hedges and roads; but with us Dutch it is only found in the gardens of the curious.

1

L. *Clematis altera Purpureo flore*
Ga *Viorne*
H. *Gormadera*
Ge. *Braeckruyt, ofte*
Waldrebe.

THE DOUBLE II MUSK ROSE.

The Musk Rose with a double flower is rarer than that with a single flower. It is a most clear and pure white in colour, with an extremely fragrant scent, [in which nevertheless it is excelled by the single kind], very sweet, and most nearly recalling musk, from whence is derived the name given to it by the Tuscans. Some call it the Damascus Rose. Others consider it to be the same as the *Coroneola* or *Coroneola* of Pliny, which he states to be medium in size, autumnal, scented, and used in making garlands. It has scattered thorns, very sharp and curved, nut-brown in colour. In other respects it is seen to agree with other rose-bushes, except that it blossoms at the end of August and in September. Further, Matthiolus writes that the more excellent examples, with clear white and pink petals, of this same Damascus or Musk Rose, abound in humid air and spiritual parts; and also for that reason, a liquid of a most grateful and sweet scent is produced, most useful in various ways in medicines; which liquid is almost scentless if made from other kinds of roses.

L. *Rosa Moscata alba pleno flore.*
I. *Rosa Moschetta magiore.*
G. *Rose musquee double.*
Ge. *Dubbelde moscaet Rose.*

2

THE GREATER AND III LESSER SUNFLOWER.

Chrysanthemum peruvianum majus is indeed an annual plant, but also a very tall one, [from which fact it is called by the Italians the "massive plant"]. Discovered in Peru and in other countries of America, it is brought from thence. Sown in the Royal Garden at Madrid in Spain, it grew to twenty-four feet in height; but at Padua in Italy it is written that it attained the height of forty feet. In the Low Countries it seldom exceeds the height of one of the tallest men; nor has it produced a perfectly mature flower, even when it had endured through the autumn until winter; and that on account of the accustomed inclemency of the cold. It puts forth a straight stem, of an arm's width; very broad leaves notched at their edges; a flower in some degree similar in shape to that of the corn marigold, but very much larger and endowed with a wonderful gorgeousness. Although its middle disc or orb exceeds a foot in width by two or three inches, surrounding it are separate petals, in a measure similar to those of the flower of the greater purple lily, but larger, of a golden yellow in colour. At length losing these petals, the oblong, flat seed is left behind in the middle yellow orb. From the fibrous, lumpy roots very little is produced. It is said that the flower turns itself towards the sun. It gives forth a not unpleasant scent.

The Lesser Sunflower scarcely reaches the height of from seven to eight feet; and from the stem arise little branches, which in turn are sometimes adorned with flowers.

152   AUTUMN

L. Chrysanthemum Peruvianum maius.
I. Tromba d Amore.
P. Gigante.
Ge. Groote sonne-blôme.
    Sonnenkron.
An. Indien Goldē
    sonne.

3.

L. Chrysanthemū Peruvi: minus.
Ge. Kleyne Sonnenbloeme

The CANNA, OR INDIAN REED.
IV

Canna Indica is called by some *Arundo Indica*, and by others *Cannacorus*, because in the middle it is in shape between a flag and a reed. It was first brought into the Low Countries from the West Indies. It brings forth flowers very pleasant to behold, of a golden and flaming colour and checkered with black spots; producing them about the end of August and in the month of September. Which flowers in shape and size are not much unlike those of the gladiolus; and arise from the reed-like stem, which is rather smooth and greenish, three or four feet in height, and of a finger's thickness. At separate places between the joints of the stem there spring up in a circle wide and partly rolled back leaves, like to those of *Acorus* or of *Veratrum album perfectus*. The root approaches in likeness to those of our common reeds, or at all events that of the Spanish reed; also to that of the water *Acorus*. In the place of seed it has as it were little rounded bones of the size of small peas, hidden underneath hairy coverings, as fully described by the most learned Clusius. Further, it is the opinion of many that rarely under these colder skies does it reach a perfect maturity.

4

L. *Arundo Indica florida*
I. *Canna d'India.*
G. *Roseau d'Inde.*
Ge. *Indiaensch bloyende*
riet, ofte
Blumenrohr.

THE GREAT AFRICAN MARIGOLD, WITH FEW PETALS.

The single Great African Marigold, or Marigold of Tunis, is the one with broad and fewer petals, in colour between gold and red, although in the upper part of a more complete and darker red. Yellow stamens grow in the centre of the flower, pressed closely together in a compact roundness. It blooms chiefly in the autumn, more pleasant in appearance than in smell; and from which fact it is cautiously asserted on the authority of physicians that in poisonous quality it is not less condemnable than pleasure-seeking,—especially to children and delicate persons. Of the other parts of this plant, [its branches, its leaves and its root,—as to what belongs to their shape], do not differ greatly from those of the smaller African Marigold fully described on a following page, except that this flower arises from a tall and erect stem of three or more cubits in height, and by its largeness holds the astonished eyes of the beholders.

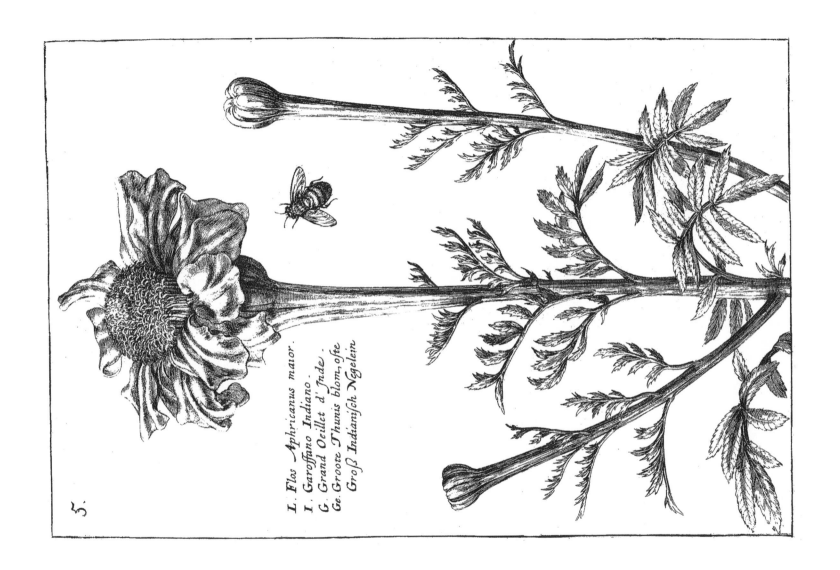

I. *Flos Aphricanus maior.*
I. *Garoffano Indiano.*
G. *Grand Oeillet d'Inde.*
Ge. *Groote Thunis blom, ofte*
Groß *Indianisch Negelein*

5.

VI
THE GREAT AFRICAN MARIGOLD, WITH MANY PETALS.

The Great African Marigold with full, or many petals, is magnificent in its wonderful splendour of colour. It is crowded with very numerous petals, arranged compactly in a rose-like rondure, yellow below, though in the upper part of a golden-reddish colour counterfeiting dark red satin. It displays itself at the end of autumn, and endures until the winter. A tall and erect plant, it rises to five or six feet in height, with branches, leaves, root and seed closely agreeing with those of the Lesser African Marigold. Some believe this flower to be the *Petilium* of Pliny, others the *Lycopersium* of Galen; but Andreas Lacuna considered it to be the *Othone* of Dioscorides. Although having some likeness to these, it does not agree in every way; but the matter would easily be settled by carefully pondering the words of those writers.

6

I. Flos Aphricanus maior multifolius.
I. Girofano Indiano magiore.
G. Grand Oeillet d'Inde double.
Ge. Grote dubbelde Thunis blom.

VII
The Lesser African Marigold.

The Lesser African Marigold, [of which two sorts are here engraved, differing greatly in beauty and in the number of their petals], was called *Tanacetum peruvianum* by Valerius Cordus, evidently from its resemblance to the tansy, and because the Germans may have believed that it was brought into Europe from Peru. Gesner, however, names it *Caltha africana* because it was first brought into the Low Countries when the Emperor Charles the Fifth took Tunis by conquest. The plant is a lowly one, with branches a cubit in length, for the most part spread on the ground. Following the grooved stems are a number of oblong leaves composed of many separate leaflets grouped together; which leaflets are notched at their edges, and, only when they are opposite to the sun, are observed to be perforated like a sieve. The flowers are in the highest parts, on stalks from the branches and from long, wide, rounded cups; with petals yellow below, but in the upper part rather reddish, emulating darkly red rough satin. Its smell is hateful, nay, I should rather say, injurious. There are fibres in place of a root, which disappear in winter. The seed is black, and in shape oblong and thin.

L. *Flos Tunetensis minor*
I. *Girofani de India.*
G. *Oeillets d'Inde.*
Ge. *Kleyne fluweel bloemen, ofte*
Indianisch Negelein.

VIII
DOUBLE hOLLYhOCKS.

Here are engraved two sorts of *Malva* growing in gardens. One bears a compact flower with a fewer number of petals, flesh-coloured, around the extreme edges rather whitish, with pink lines or little rods mingling at their centres; a not inelegant variety. But the other flower is fuller, of a red colour in some degree similar to that of the purple-red or greater red peonies. In both sorts the stem is straight, and rises to six or seven feet; from which stem hang fairly large, cleft leaves, saw-like at their edges, and ending with a point. When the petals have fallen from the flowers, or roses, a broad seed is observed like in shape to small cheeses, [from which this plant is called *Keeskens cruyt* by the Dutch]; and gathered together in pods, which pods when mature perish from the stem or branch. Notwithstanding that, in the following year the plant is produced from the seed, and at length the flower bursts forth in the autumn. It has a long root, somewhat thick and whitish, and pliant; going deeply into the ground, and producing a new stem, and branches and leaves, again in the coming year.

L. *Malua rosea multiplex.*
I. *Malua magiore.*
G. *Rose d'outer mer double.*
Gt. *Dubbel Winterrosen.*

.8.

IX
THE CURLED MALLOW.

Malva crispa is so called from its braided leaves, but was named *lancinata* by Cordus; and by others *Malva crustati oris*. Although recorded among the wild mallows, nevertheless it is seldom seen growing except in cultivated places and in gardens. It rises aloft with a straight stem, and has somewhat rounded leaves full of curves, smooth, of a pale green, with their margins notched, or rather, curled. In autumn it produces small flowers, dull white and somewhat reddish in colour. Its roots are many, by no means large, and of lesser thickness than those of the garden mallows. But of what use the mallow is, and how necessary in the life of men, not only the college of physicians but also the notable sayings of our most ancient poets abundantly teach us; and especially that line of Hesiod:

"What great blessedness there is in a diet on mallows and squills."

L. *Malua crispa.*
I. *Malua crespo.*
G. *Maulue crespu.*
Ge. *Gecronckelde Malue.*
    Krauß Pappelen.

THE LESSER RICINUS.

Ricinus was called by the Greeks Κρότωμ, and by the Egyptians [among whom, even today it grows abundantly] *kiki*, a name received from a likeness to the ticks of an animal. Tall in size is this plant; in a short time arising to the height of a small fig-tree; having a trunk of the height of a man of middle stature. Which trunk is slightly broad, hollowed in a reed-like fashion, and knotty; from which spring forth branches from separate places in the knots, of a black-purple in colour. At the top of these branches hang large leaves, star-like in shape, oblong, notched, ending with a point, darker than the leek in colour, and somewhat like those of the fig-tree but longer and smoother. From other nine-inch branches are produced little flowers close together like a bunch of grapes, somewhat greenish and quince-coloured, and apt to fall. The fruit has a livid colour on the outside, marked with interming ling spots; and on the inside is filled with a clear white pith. The seed is in a three-fold covering armed with soft prickles; and when one of these prickles is drawn out from the rind it closely resembles an insect, as I have said. The root is manifold, and made up of many fibres jointed together.

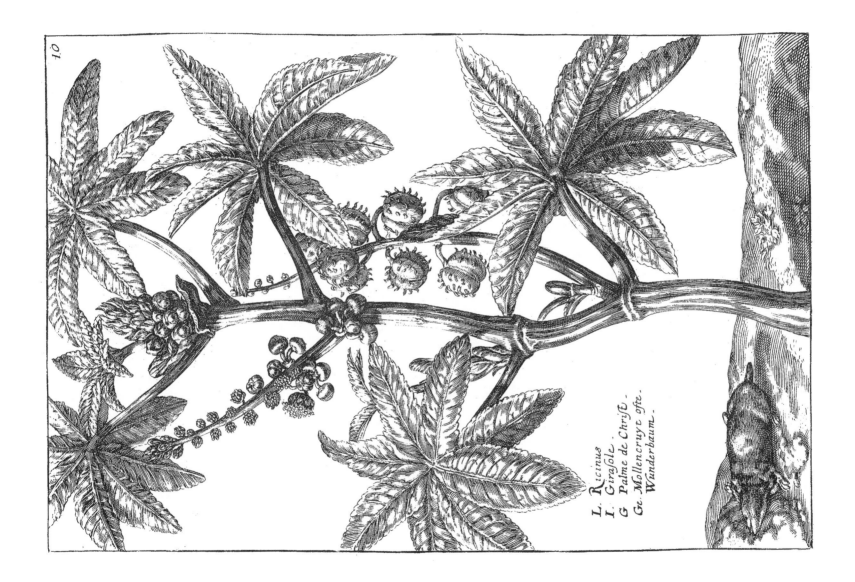

L. Ricinus
I. Girasole .
G. Palme de Christ .
Ge. Mollencruyt ofte .
Wunderbaum .

XI
THE MARVEL OF PERU.

This plant, growing in their country, is called *Hachal Indi* by the Peruvians, and by us *Admirabilis peruana*. It puts forth a stem a cubit high, though sometimes more, of a thumb's width, full of sap, strong, a yellowish-green in colour, and divided into abundant little knotty branches; also double leaves on separate jointed branchlets, always growing opposite one another, like the leaves of *Siliquastrum*, full of sap, wide at the base and pointed at the ends. The flowers at the ends of stalks are separate, "with wings",* oblong, hollow, wrapped together in five folds before they open; and ending in blunt angles at the edges as in the flowers of the convolvulus; also with more splendid flowers than those of the tobacco plant. Sometimes they are gay with a very fine purple or scarlet, now and then golden or somewhat whitish, but more often very bright with two colours. Some have the middle part of the flower filled with purple; or the whole flower intersected by stripes; or the whole separated with alternate rays, now golden, now purple; or sometimes with large, at other times with very small, purple spots. They are also bedecked with rather long stamens and a stile a little longer, emerging from the centre of the flower. The flowers are very apt to fall, nor do they last beyond one day; nevertheless this plant is wont to be luxuriant in the abundance of its flowers, continuously from July until October.

* [Note—Without doubt, this has reference to the spaces left on either side of the flower. Compare the left-hand top flower in the plate]

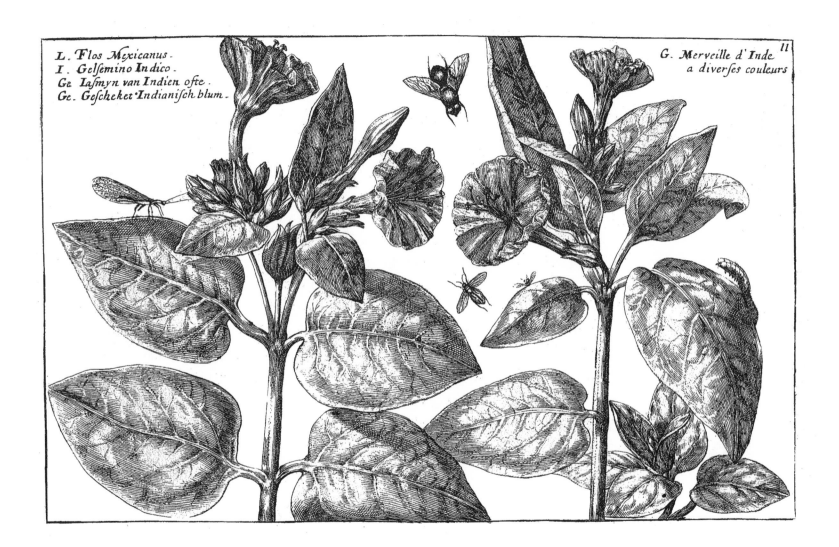

L. *Flos Mexicanus.*
I. *Gelsemino Indico.*
Ge. *Iasmyn van Indien ofte.*
Ge. *Gescheket Indianisch blum.*

G. *Merveille d'Inde*
a diverses couleurs

11

XII
THE TOBACCO PLANT.

This plant of ours is called *Petum peruvianum latifolium* in distinction from the smaller sort with narrower leaves; by some called the male plant because it is meet and held to be of greater value. Most commonly this is an annual plant, yet nevertheless it is a tall one, for it rises to so much as five or sometimes six feet; having a rather strong stem, hairy with a soft and whitish down, throughout which in turn are spread out here and there leaves larger than those of *Dyoscyamus flavus*, but not much unlike those of *Lapathus*, though broader, softer, of a paler green, with a fine down or as it were hairiness, and moreover, closely adhering to the stems as though embracing them. The top of the stem is divided into curved branch-lets which bear little cups ending in five rather firm spikes, in which to—wards the autumn blossom hollow flowers of a pallid purple, though around the outer edges almost a dull white, and ending in five pointed corners. Little rounded heads containing somewhat golden-coloured seed follow the flowers. The root is rather broad, and divided into many smaller shoots.

12

L. Hyoscyamus Peruvianus.
I. Negotiano.
G. Nicotiane.
Ge. Taback ofte.
Bilfen cruyt van Peru.

The Italian Cyclamen with Rounded Leaves.

XIII

The Italian Cyclamen, which is also called by some the Roman Cyclamen because it is more frequently found in the neighbourhood of Rome, from a rounded root like that of a turnip, provided with slender blackish fibres, brings forth many leaves almost circular, or rather, heart-shaped, about a hand's breadth in size, and lightly notched at the edges. The upper surfaces of the leaves are pleasant in diversity,—now of a lighter now a darker green [nevertheless the middle part tends to blackness]; the under surfaces being uniformly purplish. The leaves lie expanded on the ground. The flowers are on rather long stalks, having one petal divided by five deep slashes so that they seem to be composed of several petals, and are reflexed upwards where the divisions begin to extend themselves. In colour the flowers are of a full purple, and of a most sweet scent. When they begin to fade they fall entire; and a little head succeeds the flower, winding itself in many spirals to the stem on which it is fixed, until it touches the ground, where little by little it becomes bigger, and is like the seed-vessel of the march violet. With ripeness it opens at the tip and discloses the uneven brownish-purple seed.

·13·

XIV
THE IVY-LEAVED CYCLAMEN.

The Cyclamen took its name from the circular or rounded shape of its root; it is also called *Tuber terræ* and *Rapum terræ*, and by the French *pain de porceau*, — not however very aptly as the root of the cyclamen is harmful to swine. It grows in shady places, largely under trees; having ivy-like leaves somewhat notched at their edges, creeping about the ground, and beautifully painted with spots, the colours alternating, — now with a fainter now with a darker green. Having also stems four digits long, on which are flowers of a duller, whitish purple, with little scent. On the outside the root is black, and inside of a clear white, similar to a turnip, spreading itself out in width; and when it dries is wont to be drawn together in wrinkles. About the end of the autumn the leaves sometimes fall, and thereupon the plant produces new ones, amongst which the flowers blossom continually during the whole autumn.

L. *Cyclamen folio hederæ*.
I. *Pan porcino*.
G. *Pain de Porceau*.
Ge. *Verckens broot met veylbladeren*
Erdſcheib.

XV
THE GREATER AUTUMN NARCISSUS.

Narcissus autumnalis maior of Clusius grows from a rounded and bulbous root, covered on the outside with a blackish rind or skin, the inside being of a dull white, and spreading fleshy fibres from its lowest part. It brings forth leaves of the exact image of those of the more common *Leucoium bulbosum*, of a full clear greenness, and divided lengthwise in the middle by a sinewy ridge. The short stem is set amongst these leaves, uplifting about the month of September a golden-coloured flower comparable to that of *Colchicum*, [and furthermore, this plant appears to be related to that family], having five or six fleshy petals, supporting as many slender stamens gable-like with oblique yellow anthers, and surrounding a more prominent style. The seeds have not yet been met with. I deem this to be the true *Lirion* of Theophrastus or the *Narcissus* of Marcellus Virgilius.

The Autumn Narcissus with a double flower disagrees but little from the first one, except in the larger number of petals, which accord a greater grace to the flower.

L. *Narcissus Autum: maior flore luteo .*
I. *Narcißo de Autonno mag:*
G. *Narciße d'Autumne .*
Ge. *Große herbst-Narcißen .*

15

Ge. *Dubbelde groote herfst-Narcißen.*

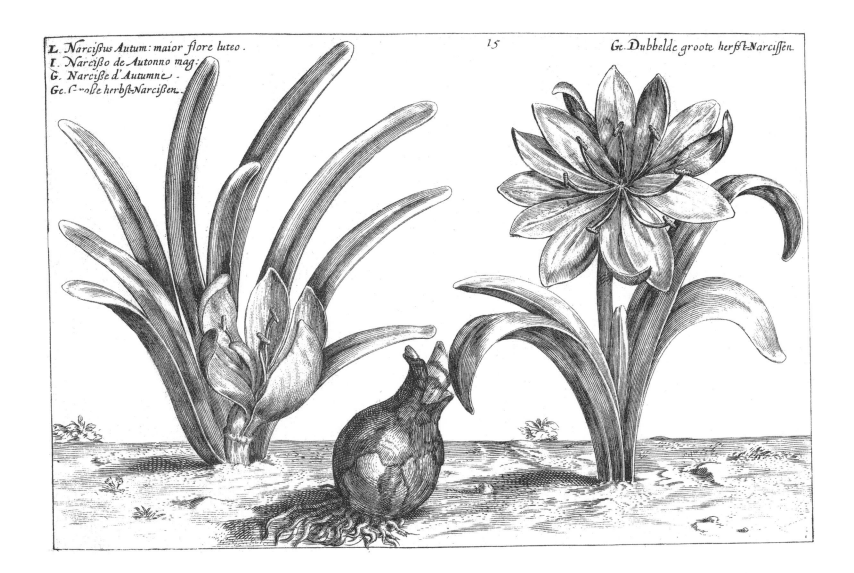

XVI
The Autumn Hyacinth.

The Autumn or Late Hyacinth has hollow, narrow, little leaves, of the colour of leek blades, three or four digits in height, with scattered little sky-blue flowers at the top, having little stamens in their centres. The seed is black in colour, and in a small triangular husk. Its root is small and bulbous. It grows frequently about Paris in France. And it begins to flower at the end of summer and in the months of August and September; from which fact it is deservedly named the Autumn Hyacinth; nor have we known it by any other name. There are two kinds of it: one with broader and longer leaves, more numerous flowers and a larger bulb; and from which it is called the Greater Autum Hyacinth. The other one has all its parts smaller and more scanty; from which it is known as the Lesser Autumn Hyacinth; its stem of full purple flowers laden as it were with berries; before which the leaves arise; bringing forth from the ground a not inelegant sight.

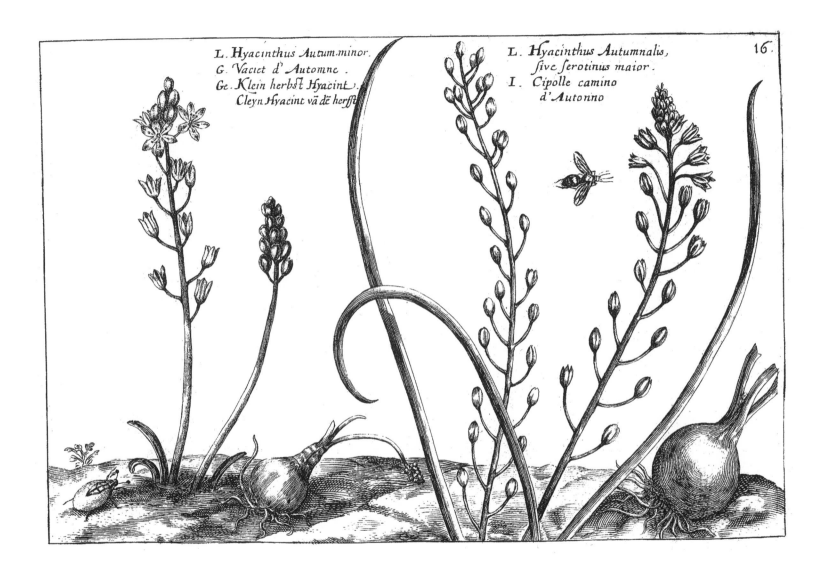

L. *Hyacinthus Autum.minor*.
G. *Vaciet d'Automne*.
Ge. *Klein herbst Hyacint*.
Cleyn Hyacint vā dē herfst.

L. *Hyacinthus Autumnalis,*
sive serotinus maior.
I. *Cipolle camino*
d'Autonno

16.

XVII
FEVERFEW.

Parthenium, called in the shops *Matricaria*, [of which here are shown two kinds differing chiefly in the flowers], grows from seed, and flowers principally in the coming autumn; and produces many green branches a foot in length, surrounded by leaves quite like those of *Anthemis*, divided by a manifold jaggedness. The flowers appear from the tops of the branches, having at their centres little heads of a quince colour, in their compass adorned with many clear white petals not unlike those of the flowers of *Chamaemelum*. The roots are harder, and ending in more slender fibres. And the whole plant has a heavy scent, and is of a bitter taste. The *Parthenium* adorned with a full flower, described by Clusius, differs little from the common sort, except that the flowers are composed of a manifold number of petals, with no, or with only a very tiny, golden disc in the centre. It grows more readily from the plant or from the root than from seed. It abounds in Britain, because it appears to be grown with skill and industry; and indeed from thence many kinds of flowers composed of a manifold series of petals are first brought into the neighbouring countries.

17

L. Solis oculus
I. Marella.
G. Maroine.

L. Parthenium ple:.
Ge Matercruyt ofte
Mutterkraut.

XVIII
COMMON SAFFRON.

Common Saffron of two kinds are here depicted: one a dull purplish in colour, the other a dull white; but save for the diversity of colour and in the root, the difference is slight. Thus is it described in general by Dioscorides: "*Colchicon*, sometimes *Ephemeron*, which they call wild onions, at the end of autumn brings forth the clear white flower of a crocus; and in its appointed time the leaves of an onion, but more gross." The stem is of the height of the palm of a hand, and bears a red seed. The root is reddish-black outside, and the skin having been broken, it shows itself to be clear white and soft and moist with a milky juice; and has been noticed to be sweet in taste. Which root eaten in the manner of mushrooms kills by suffocation. The bulb has a cleft in its middle, from which the flowers spring forth. Dodoens writes that the leaves and seed come first; and lacking these at the end of the autumn many flowers are put forth from tender stems, bare and without the adornment of leaves. Also Valerius Cordus describes the root of the white saffron to be always of a clear white, and harmless.

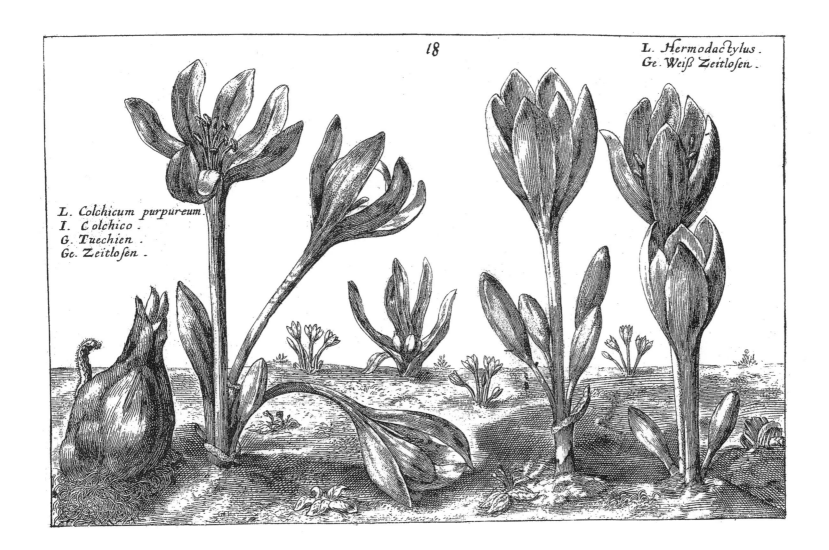

18

L. Hermodactylus.
Ge. Weiß Zeitlosen.

L. Colchicum purpureum.
I. Colchico.
G. Tuechien.
Ge. Zeitlosen.

THE SAFFRON OF CONSTANTINOPLE. XIX THE PORTUGUESE CHECKERED SAFFRON.

The broad-leaved Saffron of Constantinople with many flowers, which the most sagacious C. Clusius mentioned as one of nature's mysteries, from a bare stem in autumn brings forth on rather broad stalks many flowers, larger than those of the common kinds, and like those of the dwarf lilies,—outside of a much paler colour than the full purple inside, with veins running lengthwise. The root is larger than a fist, from whence in the spring there begin to appear three or four large leaves, wrapped round one another like the leaves of *Veratrum* but of a deeper green.

The accompanying Portuguese Saffron has a flower not so much unlike that of the Constantinople one, except that it is smaller, and checkered like that of *Fritillaria*, or as it were diffusely parti-coloured with reddish spots, wonderfully drawing the eyes of the beholders to it by its delightful design; although with very little or no scent.

19

L. *Colchicum Byzantinū multiflorum.*
Ge. *Colchicum van Constant met*
brede bladeren.

L. *Colchicum lusitanic: reticulatum.*
Ge. *Portugaelsche Colchicum fritillare gelyck.*

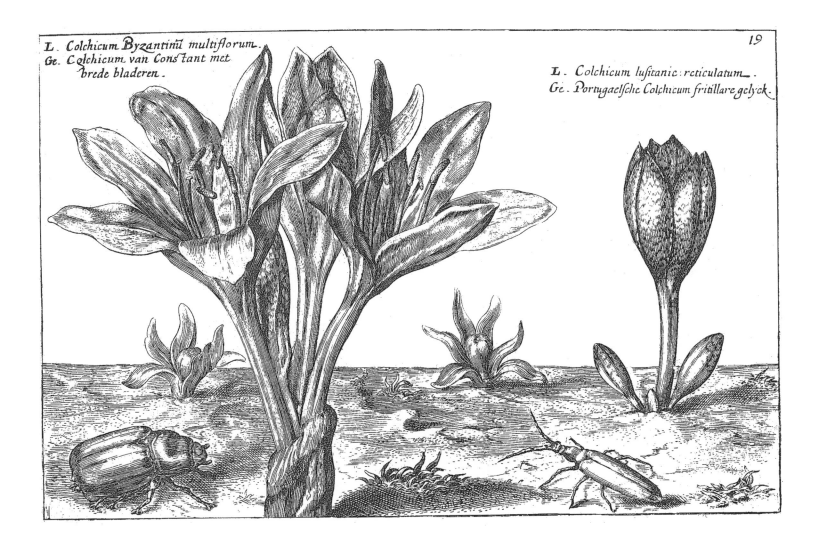

XX
THE PARTI-COLOURED SAFFRON. MOUNTAIN SAFFRON. PORTUGUESE SAFFRON.

The Saffron with a parti-coloured flower has a large root, and planted after the others, brings forth from a short stem close to the ground three or four flowers, with more rounded and diffused petals, of which the three inner ones are reddish-purple, and the remaining ones on the outside retain a milky whiteness, although varied inwardly with mingling rays and spots of a violet or scarlet colour. The Spanish Mountain Saffron differs from this one, for in September it produces a flower with six somewhat long and narrow petals of a reddish-purple, which is followed by three or four keeled leaves of the length of a finger, bestrewing themselves upon the ground, at first bright with a full green colour, then resembling a red colour which lasts continuously throughout the winter until May of the following year; at which time the globular yellow seed ripens. However, it has a bulbous root, clad in a coat of a nut-brown colour; the inside being dull white, solid and sweet. Neither does the late Portuguese Saffron agree in every way with that one; having a somewhat whitish and clear-shining flower marked at the upper edges with scarlet; for the rest it is near to the Constantinople one.

20

L. Colchicum hispanicum montanum.
Ge. Spaensch Berch Colchicum.

L. Colchicum flore versicolore.
Ge. Colchicum met verscheide vervige bloemē.

L. Colchicum lusitan: serotinum.
Ge. Spade portugaelsche Colchicum.

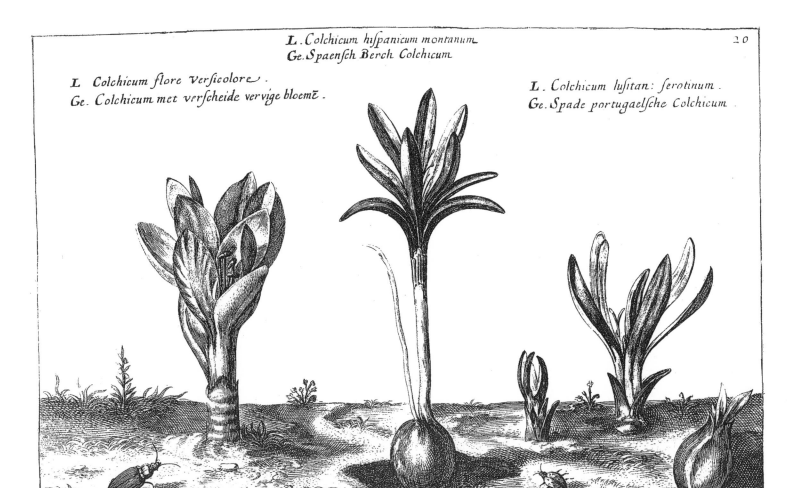

XXI
THE DUSKY-COLOURED SPANISH HYACINTH. THE WINTER HYACINTH.

The Dusky-coloured Spanish Hyacinth is composed of five or six rather long leaves,—keeled, full of sap, from ash-colour to green, flexible, rounded and pointed at the tips, with a clear white line extending lengthwise on the inside. The foot-high stem from the centre of the leaves brings forth ten, twelve or more flowers at intervals, facing downwards, and having no scent; almost like those of the Dutch Hyacinth, or to the *non scriptus*" of Dodoens; the colour being somewhat dusky,—of a purple and pale green mixed together. Black, gristle-like, flat, and almost circular seed is borne in little heads. The spherical and rounded root is wrapped in many clear white coats, and is provided with numerous fibres in the lower part. The plant springs up from seed, and preserves its leaves throughout the autumn. The Eastern Winter Hyacinth agrees for the most part with the white Eastern Hyacinth; but it grows forth from the ground in winter, raising its stem through the snow. It has leaves full of sap, and almost always straight. About the end of December it bears flowers of a lovely clear white colour, though at their opening somewhat purplish a little way around their edges. The root is bulbous, clear white inside, and covered outside with a somewhat reddish colour.

21

L. Hyacinthus Hisp : obsoletior

Ge Wynterschen witten orientael
Hyacinth .
L . Hyacinthus brumalis . lobely

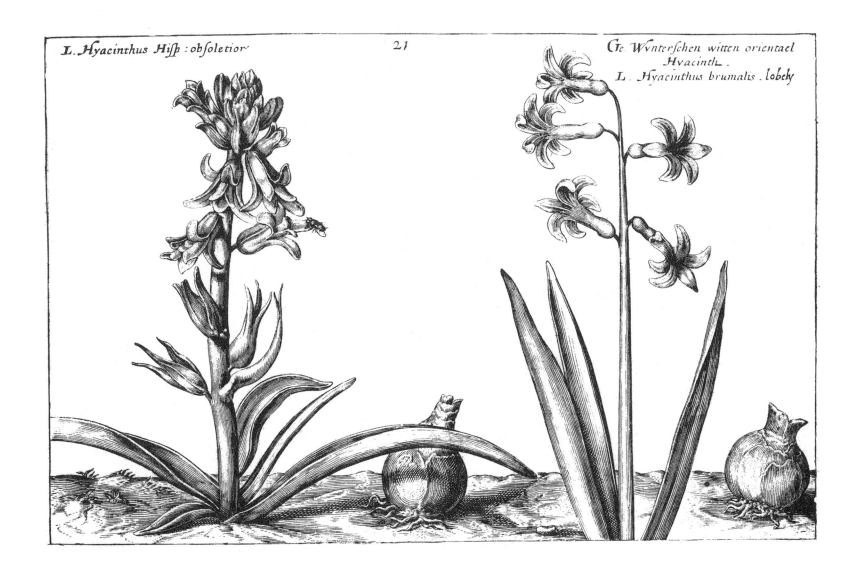

XXII
THE NAPLES SAFFRON. THE SAFFRON WITH MANY PETALS.

Colchicum is so called from the region of Colchis, where it grows very abundantly. There are many varieties of this plant, either by craft, or by change of place or climate; among which is one with higher petals, as shown in this present engraving. The flowers of the Naples Saffron may be of a paler or of a fuller violet colour, as in the common variety; nevertheless they have longer petals, clear-shining if beheld against the sun, and checkered, like *Fritillaria*, with the colour of a flame of fire.

The Saffron with many petals, rejoicing in a somewhat fuller flower, [brought from Germany, and described in the delightful garden of Count Arenberg by the most learned Clusius], bears a flower not very much different in colour to the common variety; but is exuberant with twenty petals closely mixed together, the six lowest ones being longer and thinner than the others. With time the bulb is said to increase the number of petals in the flowers.

22

L. Colchicum Neapolitanum.
Ge. Colchicum van Napels.

L. Colchicum polyphyllantes
Ge. Dubbel-bloemige Colchicum.

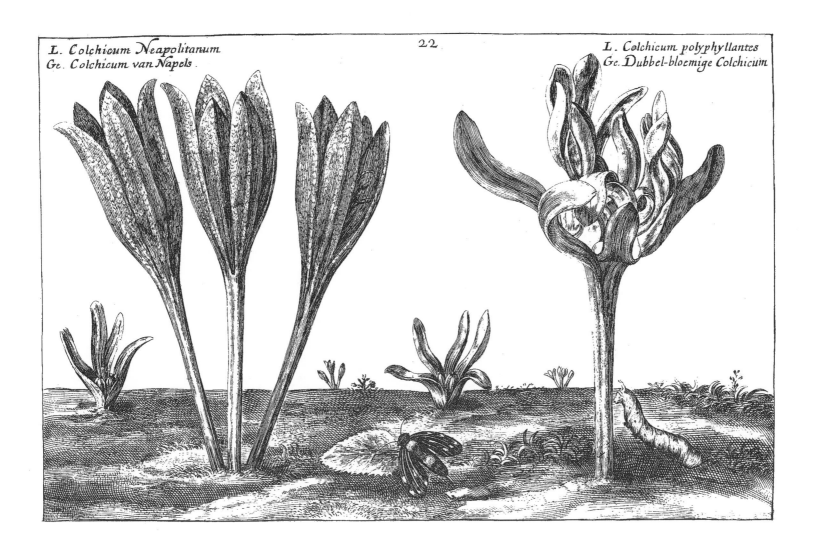

CULTIVATED SAFFRON. XXIII   MOUNTAIN SAFFRON.

The leaves of the Cultivated Saffron are rather long and very narrow; the flowers beautiful with a dark blue-purple colour, like those of *Colchicum* but brilliant with a fuller tint. In each flower are three or four stigmas, placed before the other parts, reddish with the colour of a flame of fire, and with a strong and heady scent; and these by themselves have come to be called saffron. The root is bulbous, fleshy, fertile and long-lasting. This saffron begins to flower in the autumn; as Theophrastus firmly states, with the first showers of rain at the setting of the Pleiades. It brings forth the flower before the leaves, which follow after a while and are green the whole winter, though nowhere to be seen in the summer. It is planted from the bulbs which have been set aside.

The other *Crocus* shewn here is one of the wild mountain varieties, and has leaves like those of the cultivated saffron, though divided with glistening white lines running lengthwise; also, it has a smaller flower paler in colour, and appearing mainly in the month of November.

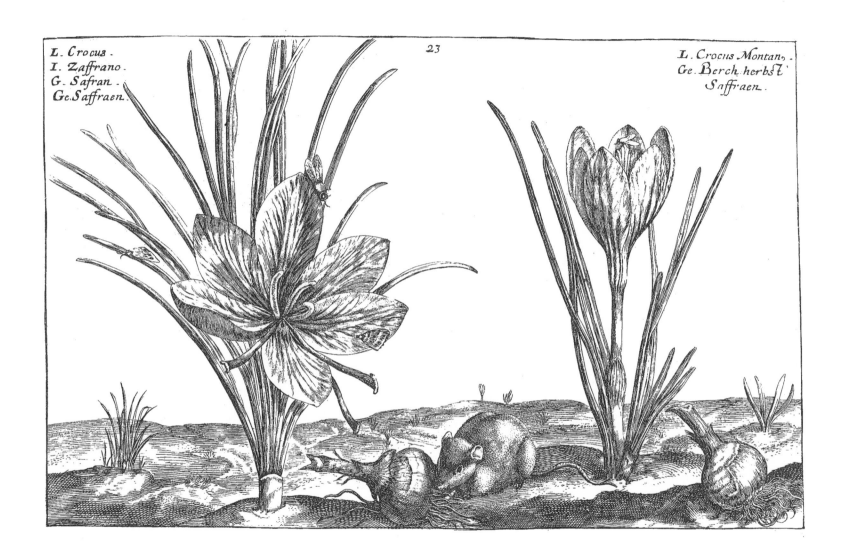

23

L. Crocus.
I. Zaffrano.
G. Safran.
Ge. Saffraen.

L. Crocus Montan.
Ge. Berch herbst
Saffraen.

XXIV
SAFFRON OF CONSTANTINOPLE. SPANISH MOUNTAIN SAFFRON.

Autumn Saffron of Constantinople [called by others the third mountain saffron], one of the wild kinds, brings forth many flowers in the month of October, which are almost scentless. The flower has six separate petals, the three inner ones not being as long as the rest, of a rather whitish colour, though in time tending to a very slight blue tint; in the centre of which flower are three yellow stamens, among which rises the three-forked style, likewise yellow. After the flowers have faded, six or more leaves spring up from the root, from a thin wrapper in which the flowers were previously concealed, a little broader than the stems and variegated with glistening white lines. The rounded root is almost of the thickness of a thumb,—clear white, solid, girt in a somewhat reddish little coat, and endowed with many fibres in the lower part.

To this Constantinople variety is added here a second kind of late wild Mountain Saffron, bringing forth a flower from a short bare stem like that of *Colchicum*, almost of a violet colour, most pleasing in its brightness and scent, and holding its beholders with extraordinary delight.

24

L. *Crocus Byzantinus*
Ge. Berch Saffraen van Constantinoplen.

L. *Crocus Montanus hispan.*
Ge. Purper Spins Berch Saffraen.

XXV
THE UNKNOWN NARCISSUS OF CLUSIUS.

This *Narcissus*, unknown to any writer except Clusius, nor by him fully described, was shown to me by Peter Perett, apothecary of Amsterdam, a most curious lover of foreign plants. The plant is a strange one, and for the most part unseen by our people; which plant protruding from a very broad, firm sheath of a pale green colour, surrounded by five or six large, broad and hard leaves, brings forth fourteen or fifteen tender little stems, each of which is bedecked with a flower of a sea-blue colour, not much unlike the flower of the third *Narcissus* of Mathiolus, or of the day lilies; and remarkable within for the two stamens, like unto little dear white horns, supporting yellow anthers. The root is bulbous, of the size of a man's fist, and little different from the root of the common *Narcissus*.

THE ROOTS OF BOTH KINDS OF CYCLAMEN DESCRIBED ABOVE.

The root of the large Cyclamen has always been made use of by physicians; and on account of its use in medicine is not commonly known. For which reason we have portrayed here both kinds of the root, not so much for the lovers of flowers but in order that physicians, herbalists and apothecaries may be able the better to distinguish it, when it is dry and wrinkled, and more difficult to know. The root of the first kind, described by Dodoens, is of the shape of a turnip spreading itself in width, black, smooth, earthy, and just a little shiny; from whence by and by come forth the little flowers each on its own tender stem. That of the other kind of Cyclamen differs from the first by its being shiny, and bringing forth very short stems, from which the leaves and little flowers arise. It is in colour somewhat blackish and reddish. The virtues of these roots are said to exert themselves against poisons.

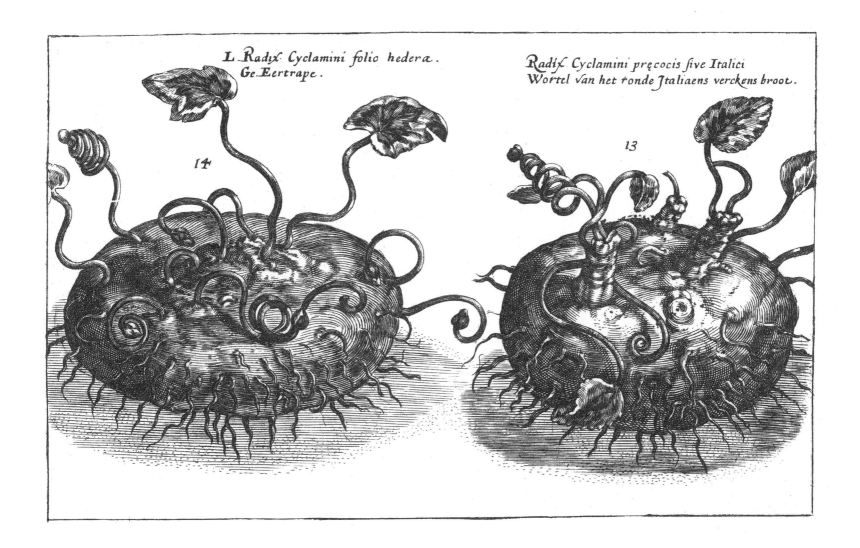

L Radix Cyclamini folio hederæ.
Ge. Eertrape.

Radix Cyclamini præcocis sive Italici
Wortel van het ronde Italiaens verckens broot.

14

13

L. *Bulbus Narcisci Marini.*

Ge. *Den Bol van den Jndi: Zee Narcis.*

WINTER

of the

hORTUS FLORIDUS

by the exertion and diligence of

CRISPIN VAN DE PASS.

MEZEREON.   SPURGE LAUREL.

Chamelæa, named by the barbarians *Mezeron*, is called by the Germans by the unfortunate name *Menschen dieb*, and in the shops "life-robber" and "widow-maker." It is a small tree, growing in damp and shady woods, with branches nine inches high; having the leaves of the olive-tree but more slender, and harsh and biting to the tongue. The violet-purple flowers burst forth in the middle of winter, and before the leaves, with a not unpleasant scent; from whence come forth the berries, green at first, but absolutely red in autumn, like those of *Arum*, and taking on a black colour after having been dried. The kernels of these berries are like hemp-seed, of a clear white, and filled with marrow of an exceeding fieriness. The oblong roots cleave deeply into the ground.

Laureola, so called because it has almost the leaves of the laurel, although smaller and unscented, is very much alike to *Chamelæa*; its little flowers also are oblong and hollow, appearing in the shelter of the leaves, and in colour a greenish white. Its green fruits become black when ripe; and they have a more oblong kernel. Also, the woody, long and manifold root sends down its fibres deeply into the ground.

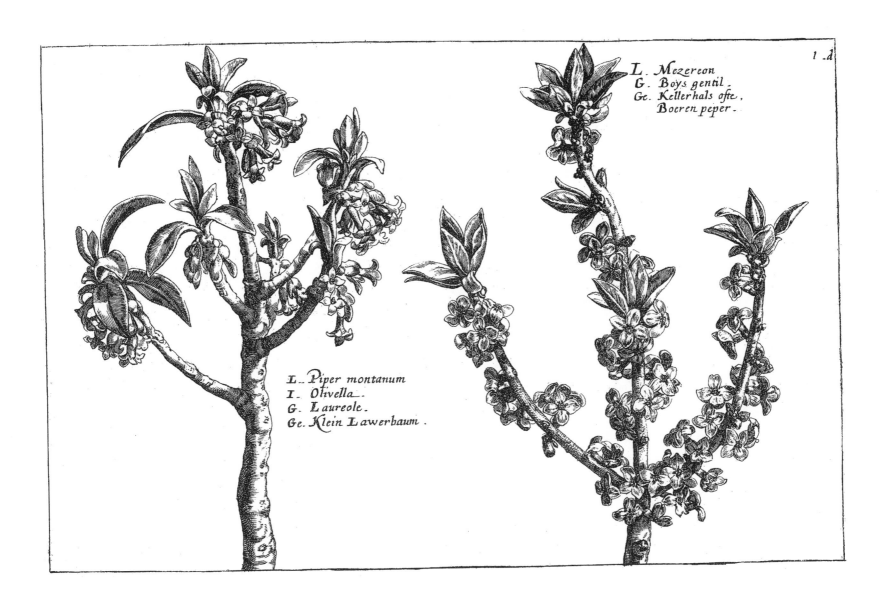

L. Mezereon
G. Boys gentil.
Ge. Kellerhals ofte,
Boeren peper.

L. Piper montanum
I. Olivella.
G. Laureole.
Ge. Klein Lawerbaum.

1 d

BLACK HELLEBORE, OR THE CHRISTMAS ROSE.
II

The first sort of *Veratrum niger*, here portrayed, grows on rugged and dry hills, having leaves assembled from many oblong leaflets, each one of which is hard and smooth, and somewhat laurel-like in shape, except that they are notched with many divisions from the middle outwards. About the end of December it puts forth flowers from the roots themselves, set on short stems, in the beginning a clear white, then a little purplish in colour, but finally inclining to a grass-green colour. The flowers are adorned in the middle with many filaments, golden-coloured at the ends, from the centre of which the seed is engendered in oblong husks, four or five being joined together in the manner of those of *Sesamum*. The roots are many, and like fibres, black, and having thin stringy fibres in the middle; and possessing extraordinary strength as a purge.

L. *Helleborus niger*.
I. *Elleboro nero*.
G. *Viraire noir*.
Ge. *Chriſtwurtz oſte*
     Swart Nieſcruyt.

III
THE FALSE BLACK HELLEBORE.

Pseudohelleborus niger, believed by some to be the *Consiligo* of Pliny, is called also *Helleborastrum*; and in many ways it agrees with the true Black Helleb-ore. Nevertheless, it has smaller and darker leaves with saw-like edges, and a stem a foot long, divided near the top into many branches, from which hang downwards flowers smaller than those of the true Black Hellebore, a weak green in colour and slightly golden around the edges of the petals. In the middle of each flower are many stamens burdened with knots of a quince-colour, in the centre of which arise three or four husks, in which the seed, rounded and black when ripe, is contained. The root also is of many fibres entangled and knitted together, but more slender and less black.

L. *Pseudo Helleborus niger*
Ge. *Elleboro nigro.*

L. *Ellebore noir baſtard.*
Ge. *Wrangecruyt.*

IV
THREE KINDS OF SNOWDROPS.

About the month of February, the Snowdrop brings forth from its root two rather long, thin, whitish green leaves, in colour not much unlike those of *Pseudonarcissus* with a yellow flower. A tender little stem, a span high and bare, rises from the middle of the leaves; carrying at the top a skin-like hood, from which only one flower, nodding and hanging downwards, springs forth, composed of six petals of the purest white, – the three outer ones entirely snow-white, larger and wider than the inner ones, which are cleft and with a green hem about the edges. Many saffron-coloured stamens and a slender clear white style occupy the centre of the flower; and skinny little heads follow the flowers, in shape almost like a green olive, containing the seed. The root is bulbous, composed of many clear white coats [but the outer one partly brown], and provided in the lower part with many slender fibres. It increases itself easily, producing other bulbs. This plant abounds in Italy; but is not to be found here except in the gardens of the curious. The early Snowdrop of Constantinople, also with two leaves but wider, brings forth a rather broader stem, bearing a larger pleasant scented flower, with three outer petals white with the whiteness of undriven snow, and three inner ones jointed together like a little pipe, for the most part greenish, but white about the edges, with green spots. The third kind is like the other two in many ways, except that it has many leaves, and the flowers by their little lines would seem to declare a difference.

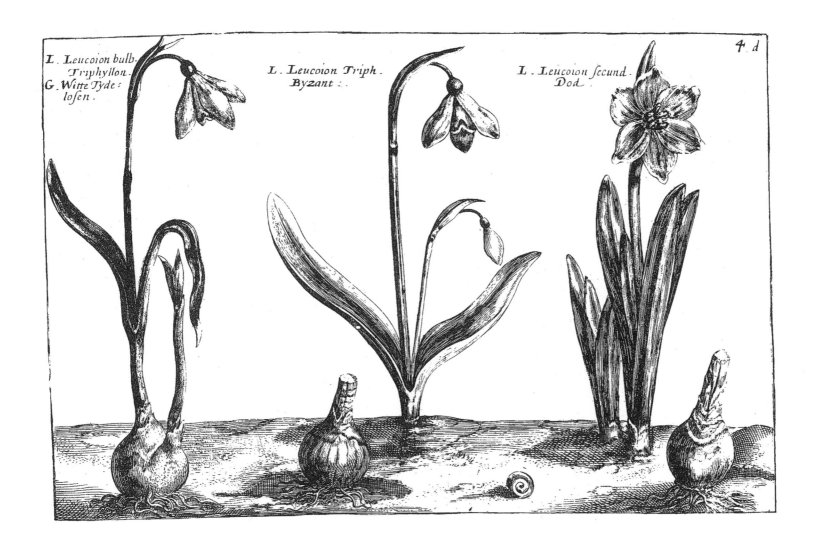

L. Leucoion bulb.
  Triphyllon.
G. Witte Tyde-
  losen.

L. Leucoion Triph.
  Byzant.

L. Leucoion secund.
  Dod.

4 d

WINTER ACONITE OR SMALL YELLOW ACONITE.

With the ancients it was believed that the Aconite received its name from a certain hill called Aconitus, which is near Heracleïa Pontica, when from the lower regions Hercules dragged forth Cerberus, from whose foam the plant originated. The Small Yellow Aconite, here described, does not raise itself very much above the ground at the beginning of the year, nor brings forth stems other than those to which the leaves are joined,—short, scarcely a span in height, and slender. From each separate, tender stem grow the leaves, which are rounded, like the spokes of a wheel, and deeply notched. In the middle of each leaf a small flower blooms, almost like that of the common crowfoot, except that it has not a little head, but in its place three or four husks raised upright, in which the seed is wont to be hidden. The root is broad, knotty, as if divided by joints, and very sharp in taste; and from it arise the little stems supporting the leaves. It abounds on mountains and hills in Italy, especially around Padua.

L. *Aconitum lut: hyem:.*
G. *Tue lup jaune.*
Ge. *Winter geel Wolfswortel.*

THREE-LEAVED LIVERWORTS
VI

WITH A RED FLOWER.
WITH A BLUE FLOWER.

The Three-leaved Liverwort [by others called the Golden Trefoil] is a herb not possessing a stem, but from its manifold root, [scattered around with diverse fibres], continually sends forth leaves, [on thin, rounded, tender stalks], not much unlike those of *Asarum*, except that they are separated into three divisions quite as though having three leaves each. Among these leaves, from similar stalks, [longer, but scarcely nine inches high, of a greenish-purple, and separate from one another], grow separate little flowers like those of the common crowfoot, or star-shaped, composed of six or more petals, and having at their centres husks alike in shape to a hedgehog, set round with little clear white filaments; and from which husks the whitish seed, when ripe, bursts forth. In the months of February or March these flowers are to be seen in joyful diversity, running riot with differences of colour. However, the flowers of two kinds are shewn here,—the first of a rose colour, and the second of a pale sea-blue colour.

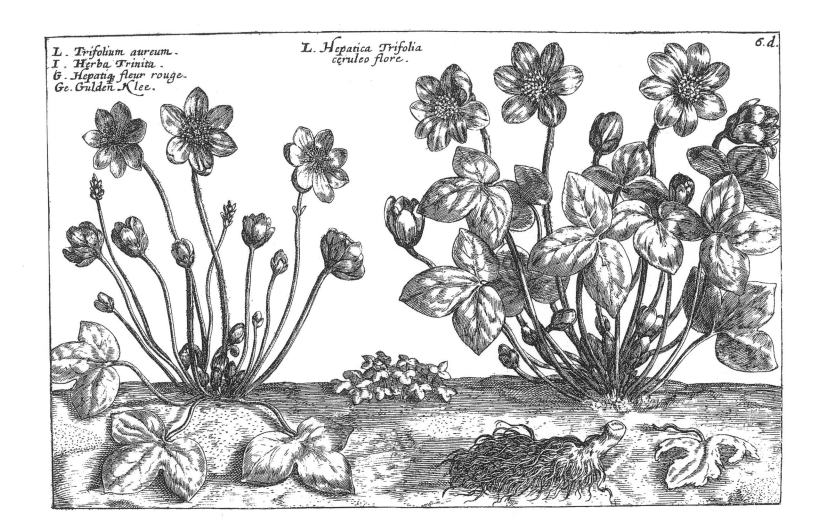

L. Trifolium aureum.
I. Herba Trinita.
G. Hepatiæ fleur rouge.
Ge. Gulden Klee.

L. Hepatica Trifolia
cæruleo flore.

VII
SAFFRON WITH A STREAKED SILVER FLOWER.
SAFFRON WITH A STREAKED GOLDEN FLOWER.

This broad leaved Saffron is found in numerous woody places; and at the beginning of the year puts forth its leaves, shorter than those of the cultivated Saffron, otherwise almost alike. It has two or three flowers, composed of six petals, [sometimes of more], with nearly rounded tops; which flowers are silver in colour, with three or more violet lines or streaks marking the surfaces of the outer petals, and contain inside three golden threads, also a three cornered, little head full of round, red seed. The root is bulbous, plain, solid, wrapped around in several coats, ash-coloured outside, of a clear white inside, endowed with whitish fibres at the lower part. Sometimes these flowers blossom with a double or treble number of petals; and truly by their graceful beauty give greater pleasure to the beholders.

The golden flower of the spring saffron, streaked with very deep violet and blackish purple colours, holds the eyes of the beholders by its elegance. It is of opinion that the more it increases the number of its petals so much the greater is its charm. Its bulb is net-like in appearance, imitating a rounded bottle darker in colour than its enclosing net.

L. *Crocus flore argent:*
violac: lineis striato.

L. *Crocus arg: striato*
polyphyllo flore.
Ge. *Saffraen met dubb:*
argentin: gestrep: blu :.

L. *Crocus flore aureo*
purp: striato.
Ge. *Saffraen met goutgeel*
gestrepte bloemen.

L. *Crocus pleno aureo*
flore striato.

THE SPANISH YELLOW DAFFODIL.   THE DWARF DAFFODIL..

VIII

The wild yellow *Pseudonarcissus*, or large Spanish Daffodil, puts forth leaves like those of the leek or of *Narcissus*, but shorter, wider and more erect. The stems are more than nine inches high, having on each a separate flower in shape like that of *Narcissus* but larger, and with a longer cup in the middle, resembling the shape of a milk-pail but more oblong. The whole flower is saffron-coloured, and without scent. The seed is in rounded, oblong, little heads. The root is bulbous, and at the lower part made firm in the ground by many broader fibres. It grows in Spain in mountainous places; and with us, transferred to gardens, it flowers in the month of February.

The Dwarf Daffodil, or little mountain daffodil, is also abundant in Spain, and differs only in size from the larger one.

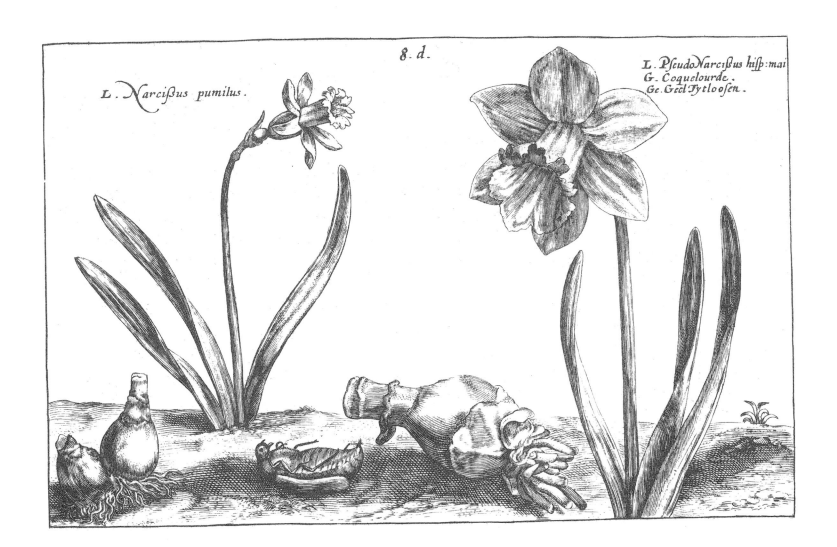

L. *Narcissus pumilus*.

8. d.

L. *Pseudo Narcissus hisp: mai*
G. *Coquelourde*.
Ge. *Geel Tytloosen*.

IX
THE RUSH-LEAVED DAFFODIL.

WITH A YELLOW FLOWER.   WITH A WHITE FLOWER.

The leaves of the little Rush-leaved Mountain Daffodil, here portrayed, are rather long, narrow, thick and almost round, like those of a rush both in smoothness and colour, and also somewhat flexible; in the middle of which comes forth a slender stem with a little flower at the top, almost like that of *Campanula*, entirely yellow with the outermost edges fringed and lightly notched. The root is bulbous and of the size of a hazel-nut, of a clear white and covered by a thin black skin. It grows wild in the mountains of Spain, and is now to be seen in Dutch gardens.

The other *Pseudonarcissus* here delineated is the least of the Rush-leaved Daffodils, having a dull white flower which differs little in shape from the yellow one, but is more meagre; and usually only one flower springs from the tender little stem scarcely nine inches high.

L . Pseudo Narcißus juncifoli, min: flor: lut:.
Ge. Geele Narciſſen met biesblader:.

L . Pseudo Narcißus juncifo:
Ge. Witte Ionquillos .

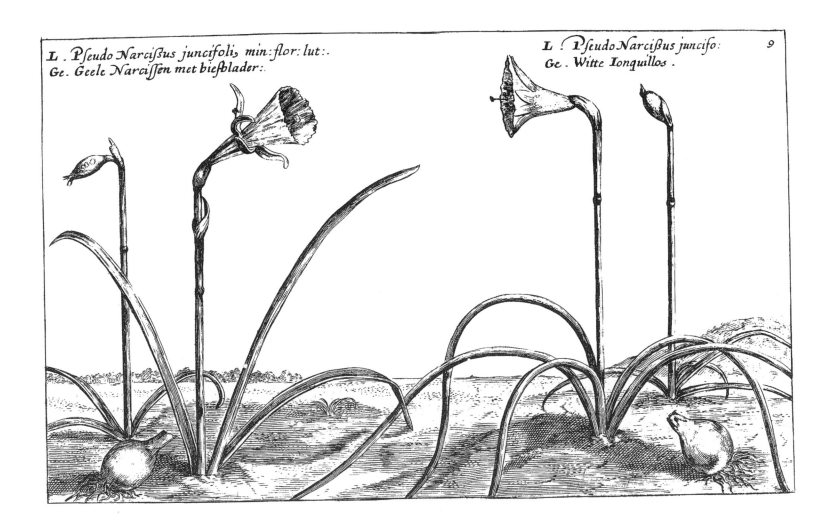

DOG'S TOOTH
X

WITH A WHITE FLOWER.　　　　　　WITH A REDDISH-PURPLE FLOWER.

About the month of March, or sooner, the Dog's Tooth usually puts forth two leaves, rarely three, very much alike in shape to those of *Allium ursinum*, but broader and more fleshy, sprinkled with many large spots of a dead blackish-purple, narrow at the base and gradually increasing in width, then little by little decreasing to a point. With the unfolding of these leaves, the flower displays itself, [supported on a little stem nine inches high, without knots and purplish], composed of six rather long petals, reflexed like those of the cyclamen, and facing downwards; unfolding itself in the gentle warmth of the sun's rays. A little, three-cornered head containing a few, oblong, slender seeds of a golden colour, follows the flower. The root is bulbous, but more oblong and broader in the lowest part; possessed of many clear white fibres, also a distinct appendage,—one only, or many. Two kinds are shown here, with little difference except for the diversity of colour in the flowers. The flower of the first is larger and almost entirely milk white, though sometimes purple and white mixed; and inside are six clear white stamens ending in dark anthers, and a three-forked style. The other kind, blooming with a dainty, weaker purple colour, although scentless, is to be commended for its more pleasant colour and markings.

L. *Dens Caninus rubro flo.*

L. *Dens Caninus albo flo.*

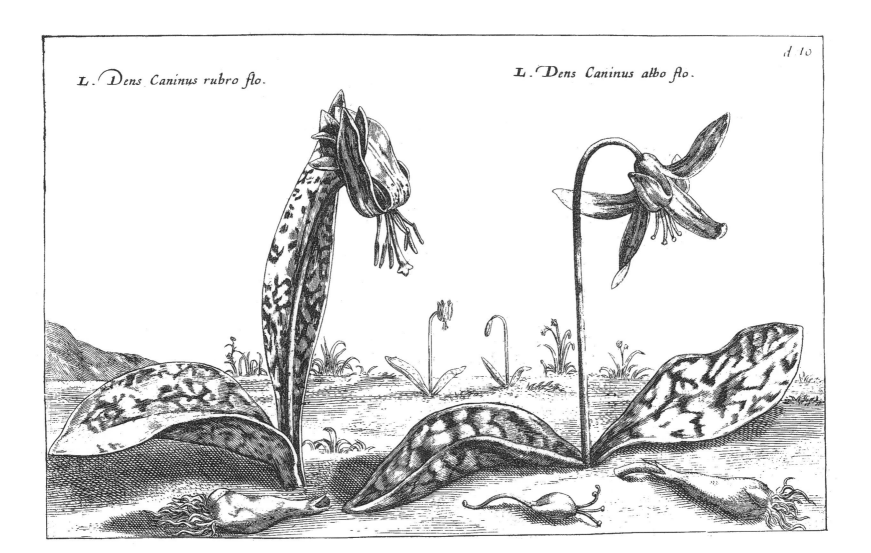

XI
THE GRAPE HYACINTH.

Here are three kinds of *Pseudohyacinthus Botryodes*, so called from their hollow and inflated flowers crowded together at the end of the stem in the manner of a cluster of grapes. The first has broader and longer leaves, and a more oblong, more compact and more scented cluster of flowers of a very full colour. The second has shorter, wider and stronger leaves, which as with the first one, are not wont to be spread on the ground, but are erect. Although its flowers are alike in shape to the first one, yet they are far more graceful to behold, and are adorned with a weaker purple tending to sky-blue colour. This kind does not grow wild here, but is reported to have been brought from the Tyrol. The third kind has milk-white flowers differing little in shape from those of the above two; but is favoured with no scent, or only with a very slight pleasant one. It has a somewhat whitish stem, and leaves weakly green and as it were fading. The tiny, rounded, black seeds of all three kinds are contained in three-cornered little vessels. The root or bulb is wont to produce many little bulbs around itself.

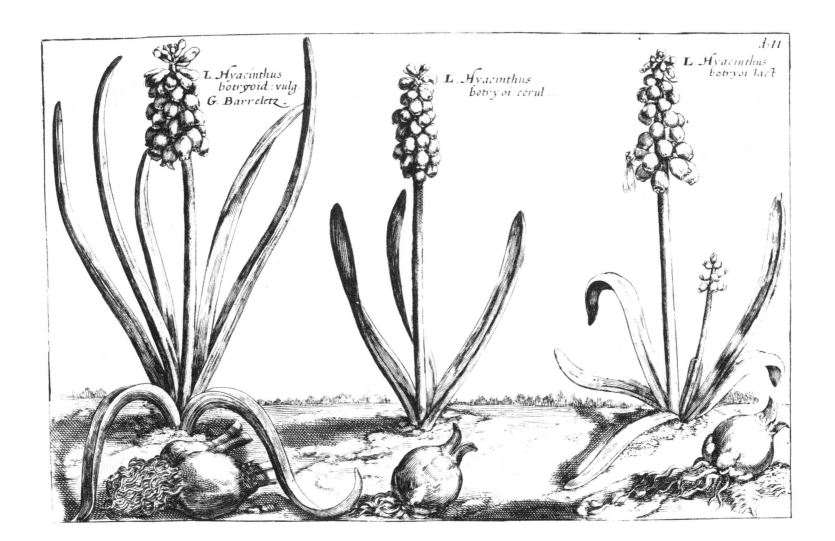

A.11

L. Hyacinthus
botryoid: vulg.
G. Barreletz.

L. Hyacinthus
botryoi cerul.

L. Hyacinthus
botryoi lact

XII
THE GERMAN STARRY HYACINTH WITH A LILY-LIKE FLOWER.
The MANY-FLOWERED STARRY HYACINTH WITH AN ASH-COLOURED FLOWER.

The *Pseudohyacinthus* of which two kinds are shewn here also imparts a grace to gardens; and, from its flowers outspread in rays and divided crosswise in the shape of a star, has obtained the epithet "starry" among those devoted to the knowledge of plants. The first, from the shape of its petals and the place where it grows more abundantly, is called the German and lily-flowered kind; and produces an earlier flower, sky-blue in colour. The seed is borne in three-cornered vessels, not black as in the other kind but only brown and as it were tinged with soot. The bulb of the root is small, the leaves are very small and narrow, and the tender stem is short.

'The second kind has more abundant flowers between an ashy and sky-blue colour, forming as it were a crown; and on account of its delightful luxuriance rejoices in the deserved epithet "many-flowered".

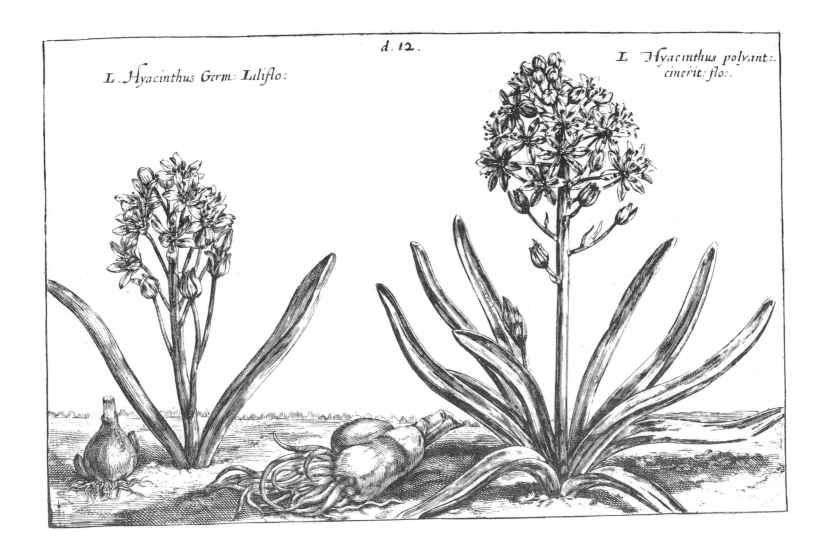

d. 12.

L. *Hyacinthus Germ: Liliflo:*

L. *Hyacinthus polyant:*
cinerit: flo:.

The Flowers